Going Home

The young man and the young woman held each other tightly. They were still, in black and white, silent, and their expressions were frozen with traces of sadness. Her eyes, soft and beautiful, were staring into something only she knew and understood. His face held wonder as if both just found out something but she first and he a moment after. Was the beautiful, young woman pushing away from the young man or was she just then, at that very moment in time, clinging to him and yet unable to meet his eyes? Perhaps in the next moment their eyes would have met, maybe with tears, maybe with laughter, and a kiss would have followed. Two figures held in a frame of uncertainty.

Keane's eyes swelled up with tears. A few of them escaped and he let them go down his cheeks to empty himself of this moment.

The photograph sat on a small, low bookshelf. He often wondered what was taking place in that stillness.

He lifted the old photograph in its fine wood frame and walked over to his open suitcase lying on his bed. He placed it carefully deep within the contents for protection.

He quickly stepped into his bathroom and washed away his own trace of sadness. The difference was he knew from where his sadness came.

Keane gripped the shining bronze handle pulling open the large, heavy doors. He removed his Akubra hat as he stepped into the familiar place. Immediately the peace and comfort surrounded him and gently urged him further in where the sanctuary waited for all to come.

Keane sat down in the rear pew and let the comfort of the sanctuary nurture him. He closed his eyes and took a deep, slow breath inward. As he exhaled he opened his eyes and looked around as if the peace he experienced was visible.

It was the presence of a thousand prayers, the hope of centuries old, and the meaning of coming home that stirred souls to return and return again.

He knelt in the pew of the spacious sanctuary of St. Peter's Catholic Church.

Keane's silent prayer was now gathered with the many here that have been given.

The door made a slight clacking noise as he left the church.

He thought about his prayer. It was a plea for peace within his embattled soul. It was a cry for home, a place to belong.

Patrick Keane stared at the river. He could see it through a clearing in the trees beyond George Street. Only a portion of the river was visible. Not the beginning of the river nor the ending was within sight.

It was almost time to be picked up and taken to the airport.

He watched the river for another moment thinking of his prayer. A prayer like a river empties into the larger sea of prayers where it is lifted up and brought back again as a heavenly mist. Prayers flow like rivers.

Life is the length of the river run.

2

A New Day

Illumination from the bold, new sun was making more and more visible the colors of the frontier sky dawning over the vastness of the ocean below reflecting the possibilities of the new light.

The airliner swept its great wings over the beckoning arc of the earth drawing the sun from its unseen side to suddenly make known what was hidden.

Keane adjusted his seat upright and looked out of his window. A blaze of sunlight ignited the sky and caused a great glimmer of that same sunlight to cover the ocean below.

The flight attendant was moving the breakfast cart down the aisle. Keane smelled the aroma of the food as it drifted toward him. Sausage, eggs, rolls, juice, coffee and tea if you like, would be just fine.

Breakfast on this overnight flight meant only one thing and that fact hit Keane like the sunlight that struck the ocean. The expectant fact was that the aircraft would be landing soon. Even sooner than that, Keane thought, we would be over Galway.

Keane tried to sit more upright in his seat as his hand began hitting the seat button attempting to make the seat move in a more forward position. Keane's head and neck were being
pushed by his shoulders to press against the window trying to force the view of Galway sooner than Galway would appear.

Breakfast came and went and Keane was sitting with his head back against the seat trying to stay calm in the anxious moments that now commanded his attention.

It hasn't just been a long time since Keane has been home. A life time has been required for this journey. What, at forty-one years of age, was the single criterion that evolved to spur on such an expedition? What was to be uncovered? What was to be found at journey's end? If the expectation of a journey is merely to be excavated at its conclusion what will be unearthed will be a broken dream lying like fractured pieces of pottery scattered in lifeless earth.

It is the journey which sifts through hidden things to bring to light its meaning and therefore the journey must have import in itself. A river finds its way to the sea and the rain carries the river in the great natural cycle back to its starting point. The river feeds and nourishes all along its way. The river run is as important as the river's end. The journey taken is as influential as the journey's consummation.

Life is the length of the river run.

Keane never troubled himself over the matter of the end. It was the going that remained important to him. The start of his journey held the most meaning.

Abraham journeyed in stages at an old age in a return to Shalom which is that wholeness of body and soul and community that would be reestablished.

Within Keane and within all humankind is that great yearning for the same wholeness.

Life is the length of the river run. And the river runs.

The morning shed the last of its fresh, gentle light as full day broke through. The sun brings its light in stages as the dawn gives way to morning and morning surrenders quickly to the full, high sun that distributes its light not in broken pieces any longer but in fullness.

This full light now brought Galway into view. The plane descended from its overnight bearing high above the ocean to adjust its heading for landing. Galway was just a landmark for the moment.

"Galway City, County Galway, just below us now."

The pilot's voice was quaint, almost tuneful, when announcing the position.

Keane had his face pressed against his window.

Thus far he had made it and thus far was a long way to have come, indeed. Thus far was filled with possibilities and excitement and thankfulness. When Abraham had come thus far he built an alter for Yahweh.

Thus far was a stage that many people don't dare to consider. Keane had now made it thus far.

Keane's right hand had made the sign of the cross and at the cross he lifted his slightly-fisted hand to rest a moment on his lips.

Until recently he had not made the sign of the cross in decades.

The sight of Galway City and the bay that hugged its wondrous shores washed away any tiredness Keane gathered from this overnight flight. The airliner took off late from America. It wouldn't be until noon that the plane would land on this finest Wednesday Keane could recall.

Keane's face was still pressed against the window even as Galway shrank back into the waiting horizon's protective glass covering.

Now over land there was much to see from the plane which traveled even more degrees lower as it descended to set for a landing coming very soon.

Galway was the wondrous gateway that Keane espied to be the founding inlet into his unexplored world. The mystical gateway of Galway visible only from the sky, or from dreams, was a fanciful notion of coming home. A vision enticed by the moment. It was not something tangible in the sense of holding it in your hand or walking upon its ground. It was more like a gesture of encouragement rather than a viable reality such as getting off the plane and stepping for the first time on a land that was yours but lost to the years like a gold coin tossed into deep waters.

The vision of transcendental Galway was lost to the horizon now gone. What waited ahead was the very real Shannon Airport.

The silence of the aircraft that traveled through the night vanished as it now raced for its landing. The pilot made the announcement. The roar of the craft seemed to build as ground appeared to be lifting up to meet the plane. The sudden thump-thump, thump- thump of the aircraft's wheels heard in rapid succession hitting the runway brought this important stage of Keane's journey to a close.

3

Tullamore

Keane made his way through the flood of people and waited for his bags to come out onto the luggage belt.

"Good afternoon." Keane said as he removed his hat.

He spoke now to the woman behind the window of the bank.

"I would like to exchange some money."

"Grand, sir. How much today?"

The woman spoke caringly in a relaxed manner.

Keane gave the amount he would exchange here and handed the patient woman the American money.

"I was wondering if you could help me. I don't want to take a car now but instead I'll be going by bus. Would you direct me to where I may catch it?"

"I wouldn't mind at'tall, sir. I'll get you to where you may purchase the ticket. We'll make sure you get to where the bus collects you."

When business was completed at the bank the woman came around to collect Keane and his bags. She directed him to wait a moment as she left to get a carriage for his bags.

She was gone only a moment when she reappeared and started to place the bags on the cart. Keane lifted one himself but she had already gotten the other two bags.

"This way, sir."

She then pushed the cart as Keane walked along trying to help but the woman's kindness took charge.

"Here we are, sir."

The kind woman stopped the cart in front of the Bus Eireann office for Keane's ticket to Ennistymon. She went inside the office and explained what Keane needed.

"Right in, sir, right in." The woman rose from her desk as she spoke.

"Have a seat here. Grand. Now, you will be needing a ticket to Ennistymon then will you? Right. Will that be return, sir?"

She had short blonde hair that surrounded the soft features of her face.

"No, one way to Ennistymon, please."

"Have you been to Ireland before?" She wasn't intruding rather just being conversational.

Keane hesitated a moment.

"Once before, yes."

Keane quickly went on to the business at hand.

"Does the bus to Ennistymon stop near here?"

"Yes it does. Very near. Don't worry we'll get you there in fine shape." She spoke with a laugh that closed each phrase.

"Now, your ticead, sir. You will transfer at Inish." She pronounced Ennis in the Irish.

Keane handed some one pound coins to the woman.

"Now." She rose with a sudden motion.

Keane stood also and thanked her.

"Come this way. What is your name?"

"Patrick Keane."

"Lovely. Paddy. A fine name. We haven't enough of them." She looked right at Keane with a dancing smile in her eyes.

"No. I suppose you haven't." Keane laughed out loud.

"Well. My name is Brenda. Welcome home, then. I hope it hasn't been too long a time for ye." Brenda stepped around the desk and put her hand gently on Keane's arm as she stayed in motion toward the office door.

Keane followed to the cart just outside the door. He reached to push it away. Brenda stepped too quickly for him as her hands started pushing the cart away from Bus Eireann.

"Now." She said.

"We'll get you to where the bus to Inish will collect you. The driver will be of further assistance if you should be needing it." Her steps were filled with purpose and she was happy to help.

"Thank you so very much. It is very kind of you."

"Grand."

It was cool weather for the summer. Keane lifted his hat to his head and with one hand on the front brim and the other to the rear he fixed it tightly on his head. Keane preferred this cooler weather to the hot and humid weather he had left behind.

The sun was in and out playing its game of hide and seek with the Irish sky.

Brenda lifted Keane's baggage off of the cart and placed it at curbside. Keane tried to help, too, but, Again, she was quick.

"There you are, Patrick. Now. The bus will be here shortly to collect you. Mind your luggage. Have a wonderful holiday please God." She spoke in short spurts but her kindness enveloped each phrase.

"I like your hat, too. It's grand." Brenda spoke with a wide smile showing her heart.

Keane put out his arm to Brenda and shook her small, delicate hand.

"Thank you so very much. You have been so very kind." Keane's face widened with a smile and returned the blessing to Brenda.

"God bless."

"Grand. Good-bye then."

"Good-bye." Keane watched as Brenda walked away pushing the cart with her toward the broad doors of Shannon.

Keane stood remembering how the aircraft approached Galway as the mystical gateway and then watched from his window as Galway sank back into its protective glass covering on the balance of the horizon.

Galway was the mystical welcome seen from the skies. Brenda was the tangible welcome heard and felt and seen as she directed Keane toward Ennis. The mystical blended with the perceptible combining both into a visible whole. That is the journey; juxtaposing the known over the unknown, hope with living, faith with motion.

The sun came out as Keane stood alone on the sidewalk of the bus stop. He looked all around him while turning his whole body around with each view he captured. He was happy. He noticed his foot was tapping out the beat of a jig. Taa-taa-tatap-taa-taa-tatap and all the way around its jagged, bouncy, winding rhythm which always brings you back again to the beginning.

"Grand." Keane said aloud imitating the melody of Brenda's voice.

His thoughts drifted with the shifting sunlight to a place further on than Ennis. Inish. He thought of how Brenda pronounced it.

He thought about the village called Ennistymon. He had been trying to picture what to expect of it ever since he made his plans.

Ennistymon now became the first stage of his journey in Ireland. He thought about what lie further ahead. .

Keane waited for the bus to come down the road to take him further into the country. The road seemed isolated from where he stood. It stretched farther than he could see and it reached beyond his own isolation.

A full-bearded man wearing a flat cap pressed down low on his forehead joined Keane at the stop. In another moment the bus came up the road and halted noisily.

The man in the flat cap picked up a piece of Keane's luggage walked a few steps to the body of the bus and lifted the handle that opened the compartment at the base of the large vehicle. He placed Keane's luggage in there and then turned for another piece and did the same. Keane handed him the last one. All this was done in silence.

Keane nodded to the bearded man and thanked him. The man nodded back and with a deep, garbled speech that Keane could barely understand the thoughtful man spoke back a welcome. Just as naturally and easily the man boarded the bus as he had obviously done many times as he garbled a hello to the driver.

Keane handed the driver his ticket that he purchased from Brenda. Keane sat on the left just a few seats back from the front. The driver was on his right. The flat-capped man disappeared behind Keane.

The bus was occupied with a few people scattered throughout the length of the large bus.

The bus coughed and squeaked as it strained to recover its motion. The driver lifted himself slightly toward the window as he adjusted himself in the seat. It looked as if he was leaning forward in a ritual movement to get the bus going again. Whatever the sound of the bus the seats were large and comfortable.

The road that stretched outward beyond the solitude led Keane onto the singular road of promises. At least they were promises in Keane's hopeful mind. He believed the road did provide promises.

As the road unfurled its curves and unfolded its bends and displayed its hills the promises would emerge as the distance took its shape. The promises may not provide a purse laden with gold but the road will stretch out to provide time, hope, and circumstance. The promises come as opportunity is forged by faith and longing.

Abraham journeyed in stages assisted by time. One step not only leads to another and yet to another step until a stage is complete but one step is also built into the whole of a journey, constructing the untouched and the unbroken search. Those taintless and unspoiled moments that are waiting to be drawn into the whole of a life pull and tug to form a completeness.

This span of the journey brought Keane the distance he needed. This span reached its length and now it surrendered to a new distance which began to release Keane from his past.

The road opened fully now bursting with expansive hues of green. Streaming sunlight brushed on the tinges of the flushed, sloping pastures that rose and fell with gentleness on either side of the narrow, open road.

Unobstructed by the lonely past which shaded his vision from the full brightness of hope Keane's emptiness absorbed the colors of the welcoming expanse of gently rolling hills.

The grayish-white stone walls lazily climbed the sloping banks creating large, unmeasured allocations not stopped by any of the many velvet inclines common to the pastures. The rise and fall of the smooth hills carved by these very old stone walls made their way climbing one atop another and then another again. The boundless rise and fall went on as far as Keane could see.

The bright blue sky seemed to be propped up above the rise and fall of the land like a low-lying tent that hung puffs of stark white clouds from its arced top. The vast sky came down quickly at some stretches of high pastures and greeted the land where it looked as if land and sky were one and only by contrast of color could the difference be told.

Keane's eyes soaked up the sights of all that was around him.

The sheep which were often at the roadside were held inside the rise and fall only by the sentinel stone walls.

All the hills and all the pastures that clung to them as they sloped steeply up and dropped sharply down spoke openly and freely to Keane. Mostly, and clearly, the hills spoke of home. This land held his very life, was in his very blood, and captivated his soul.

The hues that outlined the pasture land stretched on and on as the bus cut its way through on the winding road.

Keane's axis shifted from the far-reaching hills back again to the voices on the bus.

As the bus shadowed the road on its winding trail it stopped at small villages that clung to the edges of the swelling lands.

A few passengers climbed aboard and then at the next enclave the same people would climb off with a few still seated waiting for a further town.

With each stop, whether at a town or on a lonesome stop along the narrow road, each passenger called the driver by name. It was the same with each person.

"Hello Pat."

The next person would climb aboard and repeat the same thing.

"Hello Pat."

The driver acknowledged them with a short yet warm greeting.

Now this went on for some time and Keane's curiosity was gnawing at him.

Finally, when the bus had emptied itself of passengers Keane asked about this curious thing.

"Pardon me. Do all the people along this road know your name? So far, everyone has called you by name."

The driver reached up and scratched his forehead for a moment while at the same time giving a good, loud laugh.

"Well," he began, "ya see I've been doing this route for nigh on twenty years. Everyone gets to know ya is all. Sometimes it's a good thing but at times I wish they didn't because I want to just drive and think. Not to be rude, mind you."

"Oh I see. I was just wondering because I never saw such a thing before."

The driver laughed again.

"Where is it that you'll be gettin' off?"

"I'll be getting off at Ennis to catch the bus to Ennistymon."

"Ah sure that's a pretty part o'the land. Well, I'll show you which bus will collect you for Ennistymon."

"Is it a far ride from Ennis to Ennistymon?"

"Not at'tall. It'll be a lovely ride for ye."

The bus went on its familiar way as Keane was lulled into a gentle, pastoral state. He closed his eyes and just before slipping off into sleep he thought of Tullamore.

The bus reached Ennis in west County Clare. It stopped by a wide roadside station. Keane opened his eyes as the bus came to a noisy halt.

"Here we go then." The driver informed Keane.

"We've arrived at Ennis. Just a short ride now to Ennistymon. Lovely and dry outside for the time being."

Keane awoke more fully as he took in the words [1]short ride to Ennistymon.' He sat forward in his seat for a moment before actually getting up.

"Lovely day to go to Ennistymon. I'll show you the bus that will finish your ride. Let's get your bags."

"I was just speaking with the director of this station, who happens to be me brother-in-law, too, and he said to sit you right on the bus. It won't actually get going for about twenty minutes but you'll get aboard and rest some."

"Oh, great, thanks very much. I do feel exhausted from it all."

"Lovely, then."

The bus came from above Ennistymon and approached the center of town from the top of the street. The small low bank of shops stretched out in two thin rows on either side of a very narrow main street. The buildings were old and quaint and the colors, if any, were washed out and the brick buildings looked aged in their rustic pale red.

The bus stopped on a corner along this slender- gauged street. Keane didn't know to get off the bus here until he heard someone mention to another that this was Ennistymon.

He jumped out of his seat, hat in hand, and took a few quick and awkward steps toward the driver.

"Ennistymon?" Keane asked.

"Yes, Ennistymon." The driver confirmed it.

Keane jumped down the steps with excitement.

He shoved his Akubra on his head and went to the side of the bus and opened the luggage compartment.

When his three bags were out on the footpath Keane shut the long metal door. The bus shuddered noisily as it continued down the street. Keane stood watching as the bus disappeared up a hill and around a bend.

He stood on that corner looking all around him. His head looked as if it were loose on his shoulders and his body stood at an angle which seemed to spin his head around.

As Keane stood for a. moment collecting himself he looked around with a clearer mind. He put his right hand on the front brim of his Snowy River hat and his left to the rear and adjusted the fit.

A broad smile stretched his face. The thought hit him with the suddenness of light. He was in Ireland. He looked around again and saw Ennistymon for the first time again.

People were trying to get by Keane and his luggage as he crowded the narrow footpath. He grabbed one bag and maneuvered it up over his shoulder by a long strap and held the other two bags in his hands and walked down the street with uncertainty in his gaze.

He decided to go into a shop that sat on the corner where another narrow street met the main avenue that separated the small, low row of shops, a bank, and pubs.

He tried to force himself with the luggage through the door. He didn't want to break anything so he backed up and deposited two of the bags on the footpath outside the shop door. He then reentered the shop.

The woman behind the counter looked at him comically. Another tourist, she thought.

Keane looked at the woman and laughed. He took off his hat.

"Hi. Can you help me? I'm trying to get to Tullamore Farmhouse. Do you know it?"

"Yes, I do.'Tis Maeve and John's place up in Kilshanny."

"Is it very far? Can I walk to it?" Keane was surely not thinking clearly now.

"No, you won't manage. Especially with your bags."

The woman was trying not to laugh at Keane's situation.

"Uh, then, uh, would you be so kind as to call me a taxi? Would that be alright?"

The woman picked up the phone, dialed and in the next moment spoke.

"Paddy, this is Joanne Haughey. I have an American here who needs to get out to Maeve O'Connor's. Can you manage? Grand. Thanks, Paddy. Bye." She hung up the phone and looked at Keane.

"Paddy will be out to collect you in a moment. He has a red car. He'll wait for ye across the street there." She pointed where Paddy would park.

"Thank you. That was such a big help to me. I don't know where I am and feel a bit lost I guess. Thank you again."

Keane started to back away from the counter and turn toward the door. With both hands he placed the Akubra back on his head ready for his exit.

"'Tis alright." The woman turned away holding in a laugh and shaking her head.

"What does that American want in Ennistymon anyway?" She spoke to herself.

"Other side." Paddy got out of the car and indicated where Keane should sit.

"Front or back would be fine." Paddy stated.

"I'll be right back." Paddy said and then disappeared into the pub.

He was an older gentleman with a worn, wrinkled face. A flat cap was pushed down low on his head until it stopped just above his eyes. He wore old, worn, black trousers meeting scuffed shoes at the bottom. Paddy wore a wool jacket which was wrinkled like his face. Underneath the old, wool jacket was a white shirt equally as wrinkled.

Finally, Paddy came out of the pub with a lit cigarette in his mouth.

His breath came out hard with a struggle and he was wheezing slightly. Keane noticed the smell of stout on him but he was uncertain if the smell was on his breath or just imbued in his clothing. It was obvious the clothes he wore were not fresh.

"Sorry. I wanted to get some cigarettes." Keane could hardly understand him.

"You're going out to Maeve's? To Tullamore are ye? Now. There ˣtis a place for ye."

The cigarette went from his dry lips to his tobacco-stained fingers and back to his mouth where he let it dangle as he held onto the steering wheel while the car went quickly down the narrow Ennistymon street.

"It's a long way out. A long way out."

Paddy was breathing hard as he said it. The words were smothered by his hard breathing.

"A long way out? How far out?" Keane asked.

"A long way out it'tis. A long way out." Paddy muttered under his breath.

The car seemed to go on forever as it climbed up hills and drove bumpily on the narrow, bony road.

Keane figured he was now deep into these far hills that drew the sky from high above.

At a crossway they went passed an old, run down mobile home. Outside the worn piece of metal with a broken window children ran dressed in tattered shirts and worn out pants too short for them. They were barefooted. Two goats picked at litter on the ground as chickens and a rooster bobbed passed them. Keane had heard of these wayfaring people. The travelers.

Paddy drove straight through the dust-ridden cross in the road passed the travelers and kept going. His eye was on them as he passed by.

The hills were present here but silent in their majesty as if guarding a sacred land.

The road rose into a graceful swell of land with hedges as borders crowned with shades of green hills.

Paddy did not change his speed at all since they left the village with its faded red brick and whitewashed buildings.

Keane heard the rumblings of a river underneath the sound of his bumpy ride. On one side he saw the river. He remembered that Tullamore Farmhouse reached above a river.

As Keane was recalling what he read about Tullamore the car skidded on the loose gravel of the bony lane as Paddy stepped suddenly and hard on his brakes.

"I knew I remembered the way. Yea, I did. Here it'tis. Ha!" He spoke aloud but to himself.

"Here it'tis. Here it'tis. I knew it. I found it. It's a long way out." Paddy spoke to Keane now.

He backed the car up a few feet to where he should have turned.

There was a large, finely painted sign above a white stone and wood bridge that crossed over where the river narrowed.

The sign announced 'Tullamore Farmhouse' to those arriving.

The car backed up enough to make that turn over the bridge of white stone and wood.

Paddy pointed the car up the road that was the long farmhouse drive to Tullamore Farmhouse.

The car started up the steep, extended length of the farmhouse road. It was the smoothest stretch of road Keane had been on since his travels began back at Shannon.

On either side of this steep road were freshly painted white fences keeping in the many cows that lazily clung to the hills as they ate or slept on the pastures.

The hill climbed out of the banks of the river and came to cross over the road onto the other side to continue its steep climb.

The pastures continued sloping up and down the gently placed hills before coming flush with the land that met the road braced by the white- stone and wood bridge.

At the highest point of the surrounding rise and fall of green sloping backs Tullamore stood proud and lofty.

Tullamore Farmhouse was a large, broad house of stone and wood built majestically above the velvet hills of green that changed their deepness with the shifting sunlight.

Paddy drove slowly up this stately length of road.

"Lovely. Lovely. Just beautiful." Paddy was enjoying it as much as Keane.

"Unbelievable. I can't believe I found a place so beautiful. I think I found the right place for me. What do you think, Paddy?"

"No better place I tell you. No better place. Lovely. Look at those hills." Paddy was glad to have driven Keane this far out.

Paddy pulled the car to a stop at a small lot just below a square of pasture that reached up further to the front door of the great house.

Paddy opened his door and stood to take a full look about him. Keane followed quickly and, stretching, looked all around him. He held his hat in his hand.

Keane didn't know from which hill he had emerged as he looked at the many that rose and fell from view.

Keane placed the hat on his head with one hand on the front brim and the other to the rear and locked it in place. In every direction the land climbed gently yet steeply with clumps of trees and hedges that appeared as darker spots of green on the many shades already present.

Tullamore, like a fortress, was placed high above the rest of the sentinel hills that stood guard against the winds and the rain.

Keane noticed the river cutting through the narrow valley below. A journey's end has begun.

Life is the length of the river run.

"Hello to you, sir. Welcome to Tullamore Farmhouse."

Keane took off his Akubra. He stood there a moment holding his bag and his hat about to speak.

"I'm Maeve O'Connor. Proprietor."

"Hello Maeve. I'm Patrick Keane."

"Patrick!" Maeve exclaimed loudly with a friendly voice.

"Welcome. Come in, come in now."

Keane entered the house and stood looking. He entered a sitting room that stretched out on either side of the front door. Four large, thick-cushioned chairs sat two and two at either end of the long, narrow room.

"Hello Paddy. How are ye?" She acknowledged the driver.

"Missus." He tipped his hat a bit. When he entered with the luggage he removed it completely.

While getting the luggage settled in the house Maeve walked away for a moment. Keane took care of business with Paddy and he left thanking Keane and wishing him good luck.

Maeve returned and grabbed hold of two bags.

"We'll just put these in your room then."

Keane followed with the third bag.

They went to the end of the sitting room turned down a hallway passed a bedroom on one side and passed the dining area on the other. At the end of the hallway she turned again and a short few strides put them both at the door to Keane's room.

At the door another short hallway stretched to one side where two more bedrooms were located.

It was a comfortable room that had a large window which overlooked the sloping hills to either side of the house.

"It does get a bit cold in the evenings, Patrick. You'll be needing them I'm sure." Maeve noticed Keane's hand running along the edge of the gray plaid wool top blanket.

They put the bags down and Maeve showed him around the room. Keane put his Akubra on the far bed against the wall.

After, they returned to the sitting room. Keane sat down on one of the two large chairs that rested at the end of the room. He chose the chair next to the large window.

Mrs. Maeve O'Connor pulled up a tea cart with decorative etchings on its sides and top and offered Keane a cup of tea.

"Now. I suppose you'll be needing this won't you? How was the flight? It was late." She spoke tersely yet with a friendliness that quickly put Keane at ease.

Keane was tired from the flight and the buses and the taxi.

"Oh, tea sounds great. Thank you. Yes, there were severe thunderstorms which delayed many planes. I managed to sleep some on the flight, though."

"I see. You must be famished. I'll fix you a nice sandwich."

She went down the hallway and disappeared through the dining area.

Keane sipped the hot tea which brought a certain amount of comfort to him. He looked through the windows that rose from just above the floor to the ceiling.

Mrs. O'Connor returned with the sandwich on a plate. Some chocolate, also, sat next to the sandwich.

"Here you are. Now. Eat the sandwich and you'll be feeling better. Grand."

"This is a beautiful home." Keane spoke to her while eating his sandwich and sipping his tea.

"Thank you. I do hope you will enjoy yourself. What time would you like breakfast?"

"Well, I usually get up pretty early. If it's too early let me know but I wouldn't mind breakfast at eight-thirty. Would that be alright?"

"Grand. That would be fine. Later I will make you a bit of dinner. You'll be too tired for going out and having a pint and a meal I'm sure." She was laughing.

"Dinner here would be great. I'm sure I'll sleep through the night."

"Drink your tea and we'll speak later. Get some rest. If there is anything I can do for you in the mean time, please let me know." She rose and waited a moment.

"I'm alright for now. Thank you for the tea and sandwich. I'll be fine now."

"Yes, grand. Alright then. I'll leave you for now. Rest well."

With that she was gone to her own part of the house where the guests did not go.

Keane finished his tea and sandwich. He put the tea cup back onto the delicate cart and pushed it back against the wall out of the way. The plate with the pieces of chocolate on it was still in his hand. He sat back deep into the chair and stretched his legs out in front of him.

He looked out the huge windows with the curtains pulled back. He took the chocolate pieces off of the plate one by one and ate them. He rested the plate carefully on the ledge of the window.

Not just in miles but in moments and stages Hope Seminary seemed so long ago.

This was the start of it all. He would be home soon. It took a lifetime to come home.

Life is the length of the river run.

4

The Terebinth Tree

The weary find their shelter in unsuspecting and myriad places. The refuge offered should be as a sanctuary where the reserve of life is stored in preservation for the lonely, the suffering, the broken- down and the forgotten. There is a time and a place for anyone to be caught within the cast of despair. The poor, the healthy, the rich, the powerful, the weak, all may find their lives change to shadows clouded dark by the sudden and unforeseen turns that life may carry.

Patrick Keane is a wearied sojourner. His soul is expended from a lifetime search for belonging. Keane is not yet standing at the fringes of a drawn and flattened spirit emaciated by inertia. Keane has an unrequited hunger to be at one time and place for which his search has sent him. To be is to live and Keane needed to be at this journey's end.

Tullamore rises like the ancient shadow of Shechem. Abraham first rested at Shechem on his migratory quest for completeness. Shechem lay as a refuge in a fertile mountain valley. Its guards were Mount Ebal and Mount Gerizim. Two ancient mountains that witnessed the scroll of history unfurl in words of hidden meaning.

For this sanctuary Abraham built an alter. The tabernacle of protection provides for the unanticipated and the unexpected shifts in the quintessence of journey. The soul is the high place where the altar lies. It is not the mizbayahkh of slaughter for sacrifice but the altar of thanksgiving for which the presence of Yahweh fortifies the careworn's rest.

The conveyance of altar expresses gratitude for the sanctification of shelter. A travel-worn Abraham came upon Shechem and found rest. The promise of generational rest was conferred onto Abraham. Abraham and Sarah are everyone. The eminent patriarch became the symbolic sojourner for all the world to emulate. For all are being called back to shalom.

Keane awoke early the next morning with the soft and gentle sun protectively embracing his sleeping body with warm light. Keane leaned forward in bed to watch the morning break.

The light danced between the large trees which were huddled together in a warm cohesion of nature. The union of tall trees gathered where the cusp of the hill began its lengthy slope downward.

Keane watched as the rise and fall of the hills became light with dawn as the patchwork of pastures sewn onto the hills displayed their brighter colors of green.

These broad patches of green which seemed smaller as the distance grew larger connected with each other until they drifted into ever smaller clumps of rise and fall a far distance off.

The last hill that Keane could see rested its graceful lean at a church.

Rising clearly out from a newly lit hue of green Keane saw a glimmering white spire. The shining cross atop the fresh white spire dangled amidst all the surrounding green.

Keane's eyes traced the hills back again from his window down the lengthy stretch of familial hills until his sight rested again on the high, white-washed spire.

The building itself was almost hidden as it sank into the last hills. The spire rising from the half- hidden church carrying the ancient symbol could easily be identified. It was a far distance off but it was so very clear standing white as hope high above the shades of earth.

Keane climbed out of bed pushing the warm blankets off of his body. He stood looking at the object which held the attention of so many through the ages. This was a great silent call for peace to come to a world expressed in pain.

This was the second day in Ireland for Keane. It was the first day outside of traveling. He was almost home.

Keane sat in the cushioned wicker chair that he placed in front of the window. He felt more awake now after his shower.

The sun was fully out by now and its light captured the entirety of all the hills in a magnificent portrait.

Keane opened the Hebrew bible to where the slight ribbon in his fingers pushed the pages apart. Keane had been studying the Psalms anew before leaving for Ireland.

The voice is ours, he thought. We speak the psalms. The voice is the expression of every person whether crying out in great lament or a pronouncement of wondrous joy.

Keane read from Book Two of the ancient tehileem, the songs of praise. He started with Psalm Forty-five. 'Racash libbey dahar tov.'

Keane read from his copy of Biblia Hebraica Stuttgartensia edition of the original language.

"My heart is astir with a noble theme.'

Reading on, Keane stopped at verse five.

'Recav "al-debar-'emet v'anah tsedek."

"Ride on in the cause of truth and for justice."

The morning was a mixture of newness; sunlight, ancient words born anew, shades of green placed over earthy hills, and a cross that rose from a hidden church.

He thought briefly about the seminary where he was professor of Old Testament. Then he continued his reading.

Keane's concentration on the psalm, like the sunlight on the hills, was broken by a soft knock on his door. Keane almost didn't hear it. The knock came again as Keane closed the book and put it on the shelf below the window.

He rose from the wicker chair and pulled the door toward him.

"Good morning. Maeve's got breakfast ready now if you'll come."

Her voice was as soft, maybe softer, than the gentle hues of green sleeping on the hills.

"Good morning. Oh great I'm starving. I'm ready to go now, thanks."

"Grand."

Keane followed the woman as she turned around and walked down the short hallway and entered the dining room.

Keane was brought to a table at the far end of the quaint room.

"Would you start with some cereal, then?"

Her voice was a sweet, delicate melody playing upon his spirit. Keane thought about the morning sunlight dancing between the branches of the gathered trees.

The woman had learned how the Americans loved their breakfast from a box.

"Please." Keane wanted to hear more of her tender voice.

"Coffee or tea?" Her melodic words were raised a half pitch with the question.

"I'll have a cup of coffee, please." Keane said smiling.

"Grand. Let me get the cereal and then I'll bring your coffee to you straightaway."

Her voice was a tuneful song but yet it had a frailness blended within its nature.

Keane watched her as she moved. The woman's movements were as fragile as her gentle knock and were performed with a sketch of dubiety within their action.

"Now." She placed the bowl of cereal on the table in front of Keane.

"I feel like I'm back in America now." He noticed the type of cereal placed before him.

"We have others if you wish. Would you like to try another cereal?"

The song in her voice measured equally with the movement of her body.

"No, no. Please. This is fine. I never have cereal back in the states anyway."

He paused for a moment, and then continued.

"My name is Patrick Keane."

She moved her hands up and together in front of her with a timorous movement.

"Pleased to meet you. My name is Pauline."

Her eyes widened a bit after she gave her name. Her reticent smile warmed as it grew on her face.

Keane stood pushing the chair back to give himself room to turn and greet Pauline formally.

He lifted his arm slowly and reached for her hand. His motions carried the intent of genuine interest in meeting Pauline.

Pauline held out her hand which was not extended far from her body. Keane's hand gently clasped the woman's hand. It was a thin and fragile hand that she placed in his firm, strong hand.

Keane felt all the frailness of her body at that very moment.

Pauline was a small woman, thin with a slight frame. She was fine and delicate. Her dark red hair was pulled back held by a thin, pink ribbon. Her arms were adorned with slender bracelets. She wore no make-up on her face and did not need any, either. A faint, sweet fragrance traced her upper outline. Her skin had an ivory tone standing out against her dark red hair. She was very beautiful.

Keane gave a final press of Pauline's gentle hand before releasing it into the air. Keane imagined that her frail, light hand would float delicately in that air once it was released.

"So very wonderful to meet you, Pauline." Keane still smiled as he sat.

"Thank you, Mr. Keane." Pauline spoke timidly to Keane.

"Please. Call me Patrick, or Pat. I insist."

Keane did not want such a formal distance between them.

"Grand, Patrick. I'll get your coffee, then."

She spun around with her legs pacing small, quick steps toward the door that went into the private kitchen of Maeve's house.

The small dining room was empty as Keane ate his breakfast. His table was set up against the etched, rectangular window that looked out beyond the sitting room to the palatial view outdoors.

Keane was content that the dining room was presently empty. He was used to eating alone and the thought of others, strangers, made him feel just a little more alone.

It was strange, though, to be in the dining room getting served yet no others were present. Keane was content with it like this for now. It was peaceful.

Pauline came back with a hot cup of coffee and placed it on the side.

"Now. It's hot so mind the cup.

"Would you care for more cereal, Patrick?"

The words barely made their way across her lips from the softness of their tone. They didn't seem to have the strength to form themselves into sentences or sounds.

"No. That was good, thanks. Is there anyone else coming to breakfast?"

Keane wondered how many people were actually at the Bed and Breakfast.

"There's a couple coming later this morning. They're from England. They chose to have a meal late in the morning. The B and B is rather slow at the moment. How long will you be staying?"

"I'll be staying for six week."

Pauline's eyes lit up with sudden surprise.

"That's a good long stay now, I'd say. No one ever stays that long."

"How long do most stay?"

Keane figured that his stay was much longer than most.

"Usually it's just a few days. Sometimes a week. They are on holiday and are traveling all around, really."

"Oh I see. That makes sense. I'd rather stay and get to know an area and walk around. I don't want to try to see all of Ireland in one day or two or even a week. There is too much of it and the memory would just be from a car window anyway. No, that's not for me."

Pauline gave a short, crumpled laugh.

"What will you be doing while you're staying here at Maeve's?"

Her words were still trying to form with the slightest of sound as the propulsion.

Keane glanced watchfully into Pauline's calm, innocent eyes. Realizing the innocuousness of her question the sudden tension Keane experienced eased as quickly as it approached. Keane wondered why it bothered him to speak about it. It did bother him, though, at least for the moment. Perhaps, he thought, it was just the anticipation of it that caused him to be unnerved.

"I think I'll just have a look around Ennistymon and up here in Kilshanny. Do you go often to Lahinch? I was wondering what there might be to do out that way."

Keane's nerves quieted down as he spoke.

"I go there often. Lahinch is brilliant. It's grand, like. I go dancing there and they have some good pubs. The beach is lovely."

She hadn't been dancing in Lahinch for some time now. She did like the beach when the weather allowed. Pauline loved to walk along the softer edges of the beach near the water away from the high ledges of large, sharp-edged rocks.

"Great. I'll be going there, too, then. I'll have a good walk on the beach as well. I know I'll be getting familiar with the pubs." He laughed.

Pauline sounded the same crumpled laugh that seemed to stumble and hold back at her lips throwing the sound back in from where it -tried to escape.

"Would you be liken' the Guinness, then?" She was becoming more at ease with Keane, too.

"Yes. I love Guinness. I can't wait to have my first in Ireland." He smiled back at Pauline.

"Oh, that'll be grand, sure."

"Pauline!"

Maeve's booming voice was heard clearly and abruptly from the kitchen.

"Pauline!"

This was a shorter cry from Maeve but just as audible.

At that moment Maeve came from the private quarters of her home. She walked over to Keane in her fast-paced, short-stepped way of walking.

Maeve always walked with purpose even if no purpose at all was ever attached. Maeve's resolute walk was hitched to the business of greeting her guest this morning.

"Good morning, Patrick. How are ye?"

She spoke loudly and confidently and with a friendliness that made a person feel welcomed and even protected.

"Pauline is a good, good worker and a very dear person. But she gets forgetful at times.

"Pauline!"

It was meant as humor but also to get Pauline to attend to the morning's duties.

Maeve could bark out an order and have a person jump to but in another moment she could have that person sit down while she made a good cup of tea along with some biscuits.

Maeve directed her vocal chords at Pauline who stood timidly nearby but had backed away from Keane when Maeve yelled her name from beyond the door.

"Pauline! Mr. Keane's breakfast is ready and waiting in the kitchen. Please bring it out so the poor man can eat a full meal."

Maeve was running a Bed and Breakfast and it was going to be managed right and smooth.

"Yes, ma'am."

Pauline turned herself around in a short spin and hurried with her quick, short steps to the kitchen. Pauline disappeared behind the doors that led to the private quarters of the house.

"Now."

Maeve turned -to Keane once again.

"How are ye? Did ye sleep well?"

She spoke as if giving orders but in essence she was a caring person.

"Yes. I slept very comfortably, thank you. What a beautiful morning, too."

Keane sipped his coffee. The coffee had an unusual taste to it.

"Was it too cold for you? The evenings can get very damp and cold, Patrick. And the wind comes whipping through here at top speed. It'd be enough to blow you right off this hill, mind you."

"I was fine. Very comfortable."

"Grand. What will you do today, Patrick?"

"I was just telling Pauline I would be spending much of my time walking around up here and going into Ennistymon and perhaps Lahinch in the evening."

"Lovely. Mind yourself in Lahinch, now. Ennistymon is a much quieter place for ye to be. They'll take care of you there. Lahinch has much more of the tourist element there and it gets very, very crowded. Mind yourself there.

"Now. How would you be going to Ennistymon and Lahinch? I should make arrangements later for you with Gerry Hartigan. He's a fine man who has a taxi business."

Maeve was already figuring in her quick mind how to schedule things for Keane. Maeve treated everyone with fairness but with Keane Maeve was more aware of his needs. Perhaps it was because he was alone and there is seldom a visitor that arrives alone. She never would have told others to mind Lahinch. She sensed something different about Keane.

Pauline came out with a large plate filled with food. Fried eggs, over easy, sausage, bacon, toast, and plenty of brown bread.

Pauline placed the full plate down in front of Keane.

"Now. Mind the plate. It's hot. Enjoy your breakfast. Let me know if you need anything."

With those gentle words spoken Pauline disappeared again through the private doors.

"Patrick. Enjoy your breakfast. There's more if you'll be needing more. I'll check back with you in a short while."

Her hand had rested on his broad shoulder for a moment.

"Thank you, Maeve. Uh, there's one thing, though."

He wanted to clear up business with Maeve.

"What's that, Patrick?"

"I would like to take care of business with you for the room." He put down the fork and knife he had been holding.

"There's plenty of time in the day for that. Now. Just enjoy your breakfast. See you shortly."

Maeve, too, disappeared through the private doors.

Keane picked up the fork and knife again and stared at his full plate.

The day was waiting. The morning was patient with Keane at Tullamore Farmhouse. The fuller day that followed would be less patient. Time is, however, a bendable entity.

Time may yield or acquiesce to a need or a situation. It doesn't so much relinquish its hold on people as it does stretch its measure. It is a pliable element. Its relative elasticity will snap back and crunch available moments together if the malleable element is not redeemed in proportion to importance.

The principle of time is to live within its range of elasticity. The resiliency must be within a person.

Time had now stretched to its farthest point. Before it snaps back in force Keane realized he had better keep moving. He needed not just to maneuver to redeem the day but also to step to address his journey's end.

The weary find their shelter in unsuspecting and myriad places.

Keane found his shelter at Tullamore. He needed first to come to a place of shelter before venturing further.

This optimal morning expanded over Keane's consciousness and he knew enough to heed its call.

He finished his second cup of coffee that Pauline had brought to him then he stepped quickly to his room. He reached for his Akubra and then thought for a moment.

Before he left the room Keane opened the tall closet door, grabbed the smaller, black luggage bag, opened it and stuck his hand inside under the clothes and felt for something. He took out a few tin whistles. He chose the one he used the most which was the 'D' whistle.

Keane went bouncing down the hallway and made the quick turn past the dining room. Keane nearly bounced into Pauline who was busy carrying the bedding from the rooms.

"Oh, I'm sorry. I wasn't paying attention."

Keane looked deeply into Pauline's eyes. Some expressions may be said in silence.

"Hi. Going out for your walk, then?" Pauline asked quietly.

"Yes. I was so excited I nearly knocked you down." He smiled.

"Not at'tall. Well, have a fine walk won't you?" She looked at Keane and then her eyes darted to the floor.

"Yes, I will. Thank you."
He paused for a moment.

"What time do you finish up here?" Keane nervously spun his hat in his hand.

"I should be done by half eleven or noon the latest."

"Maybe I'll see you before you go. I'm not sure where this walk will bring me. I'll be heading into Ennistymon later this afternoon."

"That's lovely. I'll be in Ennistymon this afternoon as well. I work at Foley's vegetable market. If you are in town please drop in. It would be lovely."

She smiled with a little embarrassment showing.

"Ok. I will. I would love it."

"Please do. It'd be fine. Enjoy your walk then."

Pauline lifted the bedding higher in her arms and went on her way.

Within a coming future there is a certain past. Hope is affixed to what has been left behind. The context of a future is bound to a past. It is fastened to what has come before it. Hope, and faith, are like the coming future.

Keane's hand was on the shining, brass handle of the door as he shut it behind him. He stood there for a moment looking outward. All about him were the rising and falling of the hills. It was the gentlest of sights.

The soft hills rose to meet the smooth curvature of the amiable sky. Sky met hill in a blend of color imperceptible by any other division than by color.

Keane stood atop the highest of these hills and held back the desire to lift his hands up to touch the arc of the sky. His hand instead went to the front brim of his Akubra and moved it up and down slightly with that motion of unbelief. Keane took the first steps of autonomy as he walked down the white stone path that divided the small parcel of pasture that edged up to the house. His actions now were a reprieve from his past. Every step current within these unused moments were a discharge from Keane's beaten life.

He was not defeated to a point where an atrophy of spirit and will had collapsed him but it was a dejection from a life lost of home, family and belonging.

Amnesty was offered to Keane in the high, gentle, sloping hills of Kilshanny.

Hope, like the coming future, was formed in the same manner as the hills. The hills that rose higher and higher to meet the waiting sky. Hope is designed by the past and chiseled into a present while cutting into shape a formless future.

Keane breathed in the fresh Irish air as he began his walk down the long farmhouse road. It was a beautiful morning. A brightness covered the sky of stretched blue that met the hues of green hilltops. The shades of color rolling downward continued to cover the ground below with magnificence.

Keane felt as tall as the hills around him. His hand went to the front brim of his Akubra and gave it a slight move upward and then a quick, firm pull downward.

At the bottom of the steep farmhouse drive Keane stopped. He leaned on the white-stone and wood bridge which led across the winding brook. He looked out, hand on the brim of his hat, the movement up and down again, and saw the sheep in the pasture beyond the brook.

A few of the sheep looked up at Keane but felt safe at their distance protected by the bridge, the stream, and the pasture itself.

The sheep ran in a sudden flurry stirred by one or another in the group which must have become startled by a bird or maybe a fox. The flock of them darted in unison to a far corner of their grazing patch blocked by the rain, time and wind-worn stone walls.

Keane felt the need for motion, too, as his foot dropped from its comfortable elevation atop the wood beam between two sturdy stone slabs.

The hedges that lined the sides of the narrow, bony road decreased in height as Keane walked on. The view widened to where he saw the harried sheep still forming a frightened huddle in the corner.

He crossed over a dirt road on the side and he glanced up at its direction watching as it disappeared over a hill that lifted behind Tullamore Farmhouse.

Tullamore sat like a crown which could easily be seen by Keane from where he was walking.

The freshness of the morning still clung to the air. A house sat in the near distance with its white sides bright from the sharp angle of the morning sun sitting in its position above the hills. It would cross over Tullamore in a couple of hours before the earth covered the flames of its ball in its ocean at the edge of County Clare.

Keane could feel the stretch of his muscles as he took the steepness of the road. All the crampness in his body and mind were being stretched out as he took in this walk to its unknown end.

His shoes were gathering the dust from the ground and he breathed in the sharpness of the cool morning air. The ancient hills bordered his walk providing a rising landscape on either side. Sheep and cows grazed in alternate fields as the farmers worked the gears of the tractors which hummed in the distance.

Birds flew quickly in and out of the hedges which were showing more signs of life and movement as the morning went on.

The well lit morning was furnished with an azure sky stretched like painted skin over the dome of the heavens.

The sculptured landscape came alive this bright sun-filled morning as Keane walked among the quietness.

It was quiet, too, for Keane. The tractor or two in the distance with their busy hum did not allow the quiet to break. Instead, the tractors in the pastures somewhere atop one hill or another added to the peacefulness.

Every angle that Keane was able to view presented the landscape in a new and wonderful way. Keane moved his body in full circle to take in all the land to remember it, to praise it, to love it.

Keane continued going down one hill and then stretching his legs far to accommodate the steepness of the rise in the next. Keane passed all the patches of green that he had seen from his room.

The earthy pastels were delicately sketched out by skeletal frames of old white-washed stone walls holding up the land where it seemed otherwise it would fall.

Through a clearing in the trees the cross lifted high against the azure sky.

Keane stopped to observe the far reaching symbol.

He looked at the sight that stood white alone in the stretched blue sky.

Keane thought of the image as he first encountered it earlier in the morning. The distant cross free from the weight of the world as an azygous symbol emblazoned on an azure sky.

Keane traveled on as he followed the narrow, bony road with the hedges high and the pastures as glaze upon the rolling many hills and the cross that rose above them all.

Descending, winding, turning, ascending, the narrow, bony road went along as an interruption in the glaze of patched pasture land. The polished squares were connected and divided by the old white-washed stone walls that were sewn onto the seems of the land.

Keane walked further on. His sight was slowly gazing across the horizon of hills when he came upon the cross again closer and appearing higher than before. This time the cross with its long spire did not dip down into the trees. The new clearing on this high bend provided the full view of the cross pushed up so clearly against the supporting sky. The spire of the cross now affixed its white-washed wooden length to the body of the church which had a dramatic side angled in the direction of Keane.

The building was also white-washed similar to the color of some of the old stones that moved across the land in an unending line sprouting out other lines that connected with other lines of old stone walls.

Keane had to stop briefly and take notice of the church building which supported the cross that spoke so loudly to Keane earlier this morning. He did not stop for long as his steps continued with more vigor.

This road led to the cross. Keane was walking the road to the high, suspended cross. On this road he didn't have much choice unless he turned around.

Keane walked on. His shoes were full of dust and his body felt the sweat on his skin from the long walk. Keane slowed his pace now as he approached closer to the quiet, small church. It was as quiet as the morning. Keane could hear the hum of prayers rising from the church. It must be at least one hundred years old, he thought.

Many prayers stemmed from this whitewashed building of stone and wood.

Keane ran his hand along the black wrought-iron fence that enclosed the church. He came to the gate and stopped. He rested his foot upon a width of the fence and leaned forward. It was such a quiet morning. He rested there at the black wrought-iron fence of the church.

After a few moments Keane lifted the iron latch and pulled open the squeaking gate. He walked through and followed the narrow path to the church's high, broad wooden doors. His hand turned the large, shining, bronze handle.

He gave it a turn but it was locked. Disappointment came upon him. He wanted to enter and join the hum of prayers so present here in the choir of silence.

He turned the shining, bronze handle again. It opened.

It was quiet inside of the empty church. It appeared that no one was present. Only those prayers of which he felt the presence.

He walked silently inside. He sat in the last pew. It was a small and humble church but the wood, stone, and white gave it a comfortable character.

He knelt and prayed a short prayer.

Afterward he got up and left.

He turned and took a short stride down the one lone step that rose to the high wooden doors. His steps were on the narrow path once again. He shut the noisy gate and paused there with his foot upon a width of metal. He stared at the beauty within the simplicity of the structure.

Some moments had passed before Keane dropped his foot to the ground, turned, and walked back toward Tullamore.

Keane glanced upward and saw from far off the highest of the hills that rose in the distance. He focused his eyes on that hill and saw Tullamore. He turned quickly walking backwards and took another look at the church disappearing from view. He looked up again at Tullamore. He thought of the walk to the church and back. He thought of everything that lie in between. This was life.

Keane again crossed over the white-stone and wood bridge that lay over the brook. The sheep like statues stood scattered in the field as Keane had first seen them.

He looked up at the long farmhouse road winding its freshly paved contour up through the green pastures held in place by the white fences. It was steep all the way up.

"How was your walk?"

Pauline stopped her work to ask. She was passing by again carrying more bedding. The house needed to be ready for more guests in a few days.

"It was wonderful." Keane said enthusiastically.

"It's so very beautiful. And very peaceful." His voice dropped lower as he spoke.

He sat in the wide, cushioned chair in the sitting room next to the tall window.

"I'm pleased you've enjoyed yourself."

She paused.

"'tis very quiet. Yes." She looked at Keane closely.

"Sit down, Pauline. Just for a moment."

Pauline looked in the other direction and gave her crumpled, held-back laugh. She sat down next to Keane.

"When I'm in Ennistymon today, how about a cup of tea or some lunch with me?"

"That would be lovely. How about at half-three, then?" She smiled with her lips parting.

"Great. What is it like in Ennistymon?"

"It's quiet there, too." She laughed a. quiet laugh.

"I'll see you in town later, Pauline. I'm looking forward to it."

He rose to shake her hand.

"I as well."

She rose, too and took his hand in hers and held it, just for a moment longer than was necessary. She looked into his eyes.

"Bye, Pauline."

His hand slipped out of hers and fell slowly to his side. Her hand stayed in mid-air momentarily before reaching for the bedding that she had been carrying.

"Bye." She made the word two syllables instead of one.

Then Pauline turned and made quick steps down the hallway carrying her bundle.

Keane disappeared, too, into his room. He stood for a moment looking out the large window. His eyes were searching for something.

The white-washed cross came out of the green of creation rising to give its meaning.

Keane opened the tall closet doors and took out a suitcase. He emptied its contents on the bed.

He put the photograph in its fine wooden frame aside.

Keane sat in the cushioned wicker chair. He reached for the black and white photograph. He opened the folded frame of gold metal and wood.

They were still, unmoving in black and white, silent, with frozen expressions of sadness. Framed in a world gone by but not forgotten.

Keane looked at the old photograph of the two people who held onto each other so desperately. Perhaps the two were just a moment away from a kiss or maybe their frozen faces just parted from that kiss. What was she thinking then, at that very moment? Why were her eyes draining of happiness and filling with a sadness? What did she know? What did he know? Were they coming together or separating?

The tears he cried before he cried again. Keane took his hand and wiped it across both eyes getting it wet with his sadness. He placed the photograph on the window ledge.

A sudden knock came to his door.

"Patrick!" Maeve sounded out the order.

Keane rose quickly and went to the door.

"How was your walk? Pauline told me you had come back."

"It was perfect. Everything I had hoped for and more was delivered." He smiled.

"Grand. What is up for you today, Patrick? Where are you venturing off to now?"

"I'm going to do more walking. I'll head to Ennistymon this afternoon, also."

He hesitated for a moment. Then he told her.

"I'll be having lunch with Pauline at three- thirty."

He looked at her carefully.

"I know. Pauline told me. That's lovely. You needn't be worried, Patrick. I think it's a grand idea.

She laughed at her own knowing and at Keane's not knowing. He laughed, too, though.

"I'm so glad you don't mind. I should have asked you first."

"Never you mind, Patrick. Never you mind."

She saw the photograph in its handsome frame covered with glass.

"Have a lovely day out, Patrick. Enjoy yourself now."

Before Keane could say anything Maeve had marched down the hallway disappearing into the dining room.

Abraham sat under the Terebinth tree in Shechem. He found his shelter there as he began his journey. The Terebinth tree provided the cool shade from its many long branches. The weary find their shelter in unsuspecting and myriad places.

Keane sat again in the cushioned wicker chair placing his feet up on the window ledge. His hands rested together locked in place behind his head. He stretched out a little in the chair and looked out on the wonderful land with the cross suspended in the azure sky.

5

Hills

The long, winding farmhouse road cut through the pastures sundered by white-washed stone walls lined along the soft green of the ground like old bones.

Keane strode with the vigor of a man released into a new life.

Walking this hill he viewed all the hills around him rising and falling in a gentle rhythm. The tops of which met the bright blue dome of the sky in their graceful climb from the broad back of the earth. The quiet peaks poked high toward the heavens.

These very same hills were the cradle of his newfound strength. The rising and the falling were the fountainhead of his new life.

He adjusted again his Akubra on his head as he walked.

He passed under the thick, heavy branches of the giant tree which grew on the upper pasture nearest the home of Maeve and John O'Conner.

The long, outstretched branches provided a protection of shade when the sun found its way out of the clouds.

Keane strode with his legs stretched out far to meet the downward slope of the drive.

He made the opposite turn this time over the white stone and wood bridge. Keane followed the narrow, bony road winding through the high hedges.

Once again he had the sudden and exhilarating sensation that he was indeed in Ireland. He was in fact walking on one of its roads. Keane laughed to himself as he thought that it did in fact even look like Ireland.

The views were sudden as the pastures spread out as if a land-covering quilt had been sewn over the centuries to fit perfectly on the bones of the earth. He was walking in Ireland. He was almost home.

Onward in the rare, brilliant sunshine Keane stepped rhythmically along the winding hedge-lined road that cut through beauty and wonder.

After some time he came upon a small crossroad. He saw it from a distance as the road became straight.

The same brilliant sunshine which lit the hues of green spread out onto rolling pastures now aimed its light onto the crossroad to which Keane was now heading.

In the burnished sunlight the broken down, old house trailer stood still with the warm sunlight glistening off of the rusted metal perched up on bricks and rocks. A man in a ripped undershirt, wrinkled trousers and barefooted stood in the worn down doorway of his only home. His tired eyes were staring bleakly out toward the same nothing that he looked out on every morning. He saw nothing as he stared into the hills.

Children played along the crossroad in bare feet and wearing clothes too big and too small for each one of them.

The bright sunlight exposed what the man in the worn down doorway was no longer able to see. The hopeless and forlorn life that held them all in this cheerless position.

As the hedge-lined road that Keane walked upon cut its way through beauty and wonder it stopped briefly at the crossroad.

Keane knew these people. Not by name or sight but by reputation. These were the travelers. Some would call them gypsies. They were taking up residence on county property much to the discomfort of the local farmers and Bed and Breakfast establishments.

As Keane walked passed the heaps of trash gathering in the back of the rundown trailer the children ran up to this stranger with the funny hat.

"How about some money, mister?" They were asking Keane.

"Where did you get that hat, mister?"

"Where do you live?"

But mostly it was for money that the questions came.

The children, at least seven of them, surrounded Keane and ran hurriedly and continuously around him firing their questions as they ran. Keane instinctively felt for his wallet without letting on he was wary of them.

"I haven't any money." He lied.

He thought if he gave them money they would always gather around him every time he passed by. Keane failed to see what the man in the doorway refused to see.

"How about a twenty-pound note, mister?"

Keane could only laugh at that request. They didn't want any coins just notes.

Quickly the children realized the stranger was not going to hand out any money and it would be better to continue playing. Their bare feet scrambled away on the narrow, bony road.

Keane did not notice the unfit, ragged clothes that sagged and draped haplessly over their scrawny and hungry bodies.

Keane stepped through the crossroad and continued on the same narrow, bony road he had been on since turning after the farmhouse drive.

The hedges were replaced by wooded areas on either side of the road. The river ran along where he walked. The roaring of the water became louder as Keane neared its course. He looked through the many trees standing near the river. Keane hopped the small wooden fence barely standing at this point and went to the edge of the rushing water.

Keane climbed on some large rocks that sat in the course of the river. He looked up on the bridge and saw the children playing. At once he noticed how their clothes did not fit them properly. Yet the children were laughing and playing their children's games with stones and empty cans.

Keane's hands went to rest on his lap as he sat with his feet dangling in the cool, moving water.

His right hand rested on a small lump in the pocket of his new shorts. He had more than enough money with which to go to town.

Keane heard the voices of the children laughing.

The roaring river tumbled passed Keane.

Life is the length of the river run.

Keane scrambled out of the woods away from the river and rushed back to the crossroad. He went to the children.

"Has anyone seen my hat?" He asked them.

They gathered around him laughing and pointing.

"It's on your damn head, mister. It's on your head. Look!" They all screamed.

Keane moved his hands quickly to his head and made a ridiculous face.

"Oh, so it is, so it is."

"Let's see the funny hat, mister. Let's see it."

Keane took it off of his head and held it in front of him. One brave child took it and placed it on his own head.

"I could sell this for a good shining coin or two." He said with laughs coming from the others.

"Gimme that!" Keane joked and took the hat back.

"Here. I'll buy it back from you."

He took out a twenty-pound note and gave it to the child.

"Get everyone some ice cream or something. Share it."
He took a small handful of coins from his pocket and gave them to a small girl standing quiet nearby.

The children were delighted and they ran off with screams and laughter.

The narrow, bony road began to climb higher as Keane strode toward Ennistymon. He paused for a moment to have a look around him. He could see a fair part of the pastures and hills that stretched out below and above him. Keane turned and continued his walk toward town where Pauline would be waiting.

The road began yet another steeper ascent. When this steep, narrow road leveled out Keane paused once again. He could see much further now.. The children could be seen playing on the bridge in the distance.

It was a wondrous landscape. His hand went to the brim of his Akubra and lifted its felt brim slightly.

He walked on toward Ennistymon. Keane had to push himself hard to meet the demand of the steeply rising road.

The narrow, bony road rose sharply one last time After a few minutes Keane reached the top. He removed his Akubra from sweat of the climb and out of respect for the beauty of the land.

It seemed that a hand from heaven pressed down and the land freely and easily spread out as the prints of heaven's fingers formed the rise and fall of the hills.

The wind blew easily as he looked all around. In the far distance Keane saw Tullamore shining like a precious stone.

Patrick Keane stood alone in the hills. He had stood alone in his life. The rise and fall of his own hills, within the landscape of soul and life, there was a great and hard climb. He felt the years of loneliness press upon him as he stood and peered at Tullamore. The breeze blew gently across the hues of green. Patrick Keane stood as still as the land.

Bill and Maura stood on the edge of the farm near the small, white stone house. A child rode quickly down the hill on a tiny, black bicycle.

"Paddy, you'll be taking it easier now."

The man spoke to the small child as he grabbed at the back of the bicycle in order to stop it.

There were packed suitcases, large, sitting at the narrow frame of the front door. The short, thin man had his arm around the shoulders of the dark-haired, young woman bringing her in close and protectively. Their backs were to the road as they looked longingly at their home.

It seemed to diminish in their minds even as they stood staring. Their home did not sink in memory nor subside in the emotional worth that a home holds. But it was smaller now. They weren't away yet but the small, white stone house seemed to go toward the background of memories bound to a specific time and now confined within that perimeter. The past was a canvas where the house was now framed. It was bordered by a marriage, a birth of a son, the farming years, and shaped by seasons of uncertainty.

"Come on, Paddy. Let's go for a ride," The man said to the small child as he lifted the boy up and off of the small, black bicycle.

"It's time for us to be going for a big ride. We'll have some fun, son." The man spoke again to the small child.

The short, thin man, saddened by the ominous prospect of leaving his home, walked the bicycle to the back of the house and let it stand next to a small, frail tree which the man had planted when Paddy was born.

The man, woman and child all stood as one connected by touch of arm to shoulder to hand. They all looked at the small, white stone house. Two of them looked at it for the last time.

The car came down the hill that the child was just riding quickly down on his bicycle. It stopped in front of the three people in front of the small, white stone house.

As the car pulled away the young boy looked out of the rear window. A strong wind came and knocked the bicycle down away from the tree. Tears formed in the young boy's eyes and quietly he cried for the bicycle.

"Abraham journeyed in stages."

The man at the wheel of the car was Father Thomas Keane. And he said those words to Bill and Maura his brother and sister-in-law.

The small child wondered about this Abraham.

Keane heard church bells ringing on his descent from the height on which he saw Tullamore in the distance. It was noon according to the church. And he walked toward Ennistymon.

6

Pauline

Pauline sat in the damp and cold back workroom of Foley's Fruit and Vegetable Market. Much of the town poured in and out to purchase their daily needs of apples, bananas, potatoes and other fresh produce.

She sat on a stool peeling potatoes assisted by a machine. She didn't mind the work. There wasn't much other work in Ennistymon. She made the choices so as to stay in Kilshanny. She loved the hills, too. They offered her peace and simplicity. Pauline was Kilshanny as the hills were the earth.

Keane walked into the back room and noticed Pauline sitting on the low, wooden stool with a potato in her hand. It was a scene that could have been from five hundred years earlier without the sound or sight of the electric motor that aided in the peeling of the vegetables.

Pauline sat with an apron wrapped around her waist with the straps reaching up over her chest and shoulders. She looked up and saw Keane.

"Hi." Pauline almost whispered with a shy look on her face.

Keane removed his hat.

"Hi Pauline, I made it over the hills." He laughed.

"Yes I see that." Pauline laughed, too.

"I'm glad you've made it down. How are you keeping? Would you like a cup of tea?"

She stood placing the potato in a large, round, metal chamber which held at least twenty pounds more.

"I am a bit early, Pauline." He said as she moved.

Pauline took a step to a door and opened it. A teapot sat on a small electric grill which Pauline turned on. In a moment the water boiled with a piping whistle.

Pauline momentarily placed her cold, tired hands above the steam. She had offered Patrick a seat which he took and sat watching Pauline warming her cold hands.

Pauline had already emotionally reached into Keane's heart when he first saw her at his bedroom door. Now the grasp reached deeper as she stood, gentle and frail, warming her hands in the flow of steam.

"Now," She put the hot tea cup in front of Keane.

"Mind the cup; it's very hot."

She sat and looked at Keane.

"Thank you, Pauline. I was saying that I am early."

"I heard you." She smiled.

"You're not at'tall early now."

"You're just in time, really."

She looked away.

"I just had the most beautiful walk I think I've ever taken."

"Grand. It is quite a beautiful walk. I love Kilshanny. It is my home."

She paused.

"I'm glad you've managed to be here."

"You haven't had time to see Ennistymon then have you?" Pauline asked knowing the answer.

"No. Not today. And when I came through Ennis to Ennistymon by bus I was only here for a short time."

"I love Ennis. It's a pretty city. I love to walk the stone footpaths and window-shop. I take the bus from time to time."

Keane sipped his tea and felt quite relaxed.

"It's always good to get home, though. I feel the warmth of the Kilshanny hills even in the colder weather." She took a sip of tea.

They both smiled and finished their tea.

"Pauline. If you have the time perhaps we can go for some lunch at a place you like."

"But I can come back, too, if you like. I know you are busy now."

"I wouldn't mind." She said shyly.

"Mrs. Foley will be back shortly and then we can go."

"Where shall we go?"

Pauline leaned forward thinking.

"There's Fitzpatrick's at the bottom of the street."

Fitzpatrick's was a modern place that the locals patronized. Not many tourists came in.

"Ok. Fitzpatrick's it is."

"Would you like more tea, Patrick?"

Pauline stood and reached for Keane's cup.

"Ok. I'll have another cup. Thanks."

Pauline poured the hot water into the cup with a new tea bag. She glanced at his face. She wanted to study his features. She thought he was a handsome man in a different sort of way. She couldn't put a finger on it. But she liked him. She liked his company.

A short while later both of them were walking down toward Fitzpatrick's. Pauline was staring at Keane's hat.

"No one wears a hat like that around here," she said laughing.

"Is it an American cowboy hat?"

"No, it's an Akubra from Australia. I ordered it off of the internet. Do you like it? Don't worry if you don't. Not many do like it."

"It's alright." She smiled.

"Are you laughing at me? Here."

He quickly took off his hat and placed it on Pauline's head.

"Oh! I see what you are laughing at now. Do I look like that?" Keane was laughing hard now.

Pauline fixed the hat on her head and turned to Keane.

"How do I look?"

The hat was too big for her head. They both had a good laugh over it.

"Well, you look like a real cowgirl now."

Keane and Pauline walked down the street talking and laughing while Pauline wore the Akubra.

They entered Fitzpatrick's and found an empty table just below the large window which looked out onto the busy street. The small restaurant was crowded but not as it would have been an hour earlier.

After getting a table Keane put his hat on his chair as he and Pauline walked up to the counter to place their lunch order.

The two of them sat at the table with the midday sun shining through the large window. Pauline's face was lit with excitement and brightened by the rare sunlight. Keane looked at her in this new light. She was as beautiful and gentle as a simple, single flower. She would never be lost amidst a bouquet of them in all the varied colors and sorts. No, Pauline stood as the single flower.

She was as clear as a poem, too. So much meaning can be attributed to a poem. So much, even, there would be no end.

Keane sat feeling all the weight of his years as he watched Pauline with the light surrounding her face. She reflected back to him a freshness as rare as the Irish sunshine. He felt his years not as something which pressed heavy upon him but as something remembered which has passed him by almost without notice. Now he sat before her recalling what he had missed. And Pauline brought it all back like a river suddenly filled with streaming water and flowing quickly over the shallow banks where Keane stood.

"My parents are in America, Patrick. But I have never been there myself. They had to leave as things were not good for them here back then. I haven't seen them now for many years."

She ate her food as she spoke.

"That must be very difficult, Pauline."

Keane looked at her with a new focus.

"I'm a professor, Pauline. Can you believe it?" He laughed.

"I can believe it. You appear very studious even if you are hiding behind that hat."

She ate her food as if she didn't say that comment.

"Well! Why don't you tell me my whole life now?" He smiled at her.

For some uncanny reason she could say nothing wrong to Keane.

"I'd much prefer to hear it from you, Patrick. No guessing. Like I just did with your hat." She smiled back at him.

"I'd love to tell you everything."

"But..." She looked at him.

"I'd rather get another chance to be with you."

"I wouldn't mind, Patrick."

"Professor of what?"

"I taught at a seminary. This was my last year. I took an early retirement. I was Professor of Old Testament."

"That explains the Hebrew Bible in your room."

She looked up at him. He was smiling.

"I saw it while cleaning." She smiled back.

"It must have been very interesting. I'd love to hear more about it."

"I wouldn't mind telling you. I want to learn more about you as well."

The conversation went on easily as they sat in the sunlight. When they both had finished they got up to walk out doors.

"Let's walk by the river, Patrick. It's a lovely day for it. The river runs through town."

The two of them walked down toward the main street of Ennistymon. They crossed the busy avenue near Crosbie's

Shop. Once across the busy afternoon street Pauline led Patrick toward the river.

They stood at the banks on the ledge of the stone wall. They looked down at the water.

"What are you going to do now, Patrick? I mean now that you aren't teaching any longer."

She spoke as they moved along the ledge of the stone wall.

The ledge was not a path to walk on but they had climbed up to look at the water. The streaming water urged the two of them to walk.

"I don't know, Pauline. The place had changed so much, and I changed so much, that I couldn't stay any longer. I'm not sure what I'll do. But I knew I must come here."

"I'm sure it'll work out for you. We'll light a candle at church."

"I've come to Tullamore for shelter. I've come to gather my strength. You see there's something I've come to do. It frightens me a bit. I'm not sure why. I'll tell you sometime if you'd like."

"If you'd like. I'd listen to you."

"I don't mean to have such a mystery."

"'Tis alright, now. I understand. I rather enjoy the mystery."

After a short, quiet distance they stopped. The wind blew pushing Pauline's hair back. Patrick held his hat. He faced her. She was already facing him. The wind blew as they looked at each other on the ledge of the stone wall above the flowing river.

They walked along the river until the ledge of the wall stopped where the river had a bend. They walked instead up the hill to the gray, castle-like Falls Hotel that sat atop it.

They had been gone some time when Keane mentioned it to Pauline.

"I suppose I'd better be getting back, sure."

They walked down the road instead of on the ledge of the stone wall.

Keane and Pauline walked up the street again to Foley's market. At the door Keane stopped and asked a question.

"How does one get to Lahinch, Pauline? I think I'll go and have my first pint of the Guinness in Ireland."

He smiled.

"Grand!"

Pauline laughed, too.

"It's quite a walk. But we can call Paddy to take you there. He's home now as we just passed his house and I noticed his car in front."

She opened the door to Foley's and the high-pitched bell rang.

Keane followed Pauline into the shop and over to the counter where Pauline picked up the phone and rang Paddy.

She put down the phone after a moment.

"He'll be right over. Lahinch is just a short ride over. You'll be there in only a few minutes."

"Oh... ok. Thank you."

Keane felt a sadness creep inside of him.

"It's a lovely day for Lahinch. You'll enjoy yourself there. Mind your pints now." She laughed that shy laugh that was a part of her.

"Thank you for having lunch with me. I very much enjoyed your company,"

"You're welcome I'm sure. I had a lovely time with you. I guess I'll see you in the morning at breakfast. Have a fun time in Lahinch."

She reached out her hand to say goodbye. Keane smiled as he lifted his hand to meet hers. A car horn sounded out front.

"That's Paddy now. Bye, Patrick." She said softly.

Keane turned to leave.

"So long, Pauline. See you tomorrow."

He opened the door.

"Have fun."

She spoke louder than she had before.

The door shut and the high-pitched bell rang once again.

7

Gathering

Paddy and Keane rode once again. Lahinch sat on the ocean side of Kilshanny. It was the seaside village of sunsets. Lahinch was quaint and clung tightly to the shore.

"Where's it you'll be goin' in Lahinch?" Paddy mumbled.

"I'm not sure of the first stop but I will be making my way to my first pint in a short while." Keane laughed.

"Oh grand! If it's a pint you'd be wantin', and why wouldn't ye I'd say, then you'll have your choice of a few pubs now."

"I see. Well, perhaps I'll just walk the town first. I'll choose a pub afterward."

"There are some lovely shops in Lahinch. Mind the prices now. They can be a bit dear on the pound. But lovely shops nonetheless."

Lahinch shone brilliantly in the rare Irish sunshine as the light reflected off of the small rows of shops on the narrow avenue.

There were only two main streets in this busy resort village. Many outlying streets lined the village proper but the resort area was confined and stuffed onto only the two avenues.

Keane stood a moment in the parking lot of O'Looney's Pub at the bottom of the main avenue. He placed the Akubra on his head.

Across the empty lot in which he stood was a path that stretched the length of the rocky beach. Keane turned and walked toward the sound of the sea. He stepped out of the lot and put his steps onto the sandy path.

The peacefulness flowed through Keane as he walked the beach trail. It was a communion of the worn-down, homeless spirit with the spirit of beginnings, wonder, and belonging.

There is a clarity in nature with which Keane strives to merge his spirit. But the restlessness of humankind cannot be driven to merge with creation; creation will bring humankind to the stillness in which clarity can be found.

Keane walked along the sandy path which distended atop craggy banks of large rocks of varied shapes. The wind was steady enough so that Keane removed his hat and walked with it in his hand.

He stopped after a few minutes and sat on one of the large rocks near the sandy path. He looked out toward the ocean which draped its bluish-gray body along the darker base of the mountains. The water was calm.

The wind blew steady. Keane took his communion. There was no Latin spoken, no wounds to inflict on differences, no hypocrisy. There was only that which was and that which needed to be.

He would try to come back here often he thought to himself as he rose from the rock and headed back to town.

His feet stepped back onto the anomalous ground atypical of nature. He touched the world which had forsaken shalom for its own devices.

Galvin's Pub stood at the top of the street. He walked to the corner and stood waiting for the traffic to give him the chance to cross.

He noticed the tall structure of the church which sat waiting next to Calvin's Pub. Keane got the break he needed and ran a little bit to make it across the busy street.

Pulling on one of the large heavy doors he walked into Galvin's and sat on one of the empty wooden and vinyl padded stools at the bar.

The smell of cigarettes was heavy in the musty air. A radio played above the conversation of the few people who were gathered at the bar and at a few tables to the rear of the pub.

"What can I get you?" The woman asked in a bright tone.

"I'll have a pint of Guinness, please."

"Alright, I'll bring it to you, then."

She stepped away with a quick step and put a fresh glass under the tap.

The tap poured smooth and dark into the clear, shapely glass. The stream of Guinness stemming from the silver tap of the wooden barrel formed a head of foam on top of the glass like a freshly finished sculpture of two-tone bronze.

She let the glass sit for a moment.

Keane looked around as he waited for his first pint of Guinness in Ireland.

He heard people behind him at a table having a good time. There were two people on the window side of the dark wood bar speaking in low tones of the day's events. There were also two young women sitting on the opposite side laughing and drinking pints of Guinness.

The woman publican brought Keane his Guinness.

"Now." She placed the Guinness down in front of Keane.

The pint glass made a solid thud sound as it hit the dark wood bar.

"Thank you." Keane said.

"That's two pounds, then." She said in that same bright tone.

Keane put the two coins on the bar and the woman swept them into her hand.

"Thanks much," she said.

Keane let the glass sit for a moment admiring its beauty. The pint glass curved slowly in the middle with the dark stout sitting within its lithe shape as the tan colored head sat majestically atop the glass.

"Cheers."

The voices came from the two young women sitting near Keane.

They laughed as they saw the surprise on Keane's face.

"Yes," Keane laughed with them.

"Cheers."

Keane lifted the supple glass while pointing it a bit toward the two young women and placed the wet rim on his lips.

The stream of Guinness sliced through the lightly bronzed head of foam and slipped passed his lips. He tasted the Guinness smooth and pure.

"Your first?" One of the women asked.

"In Ireland." Keane spoke.

He took another thirsty sip.

"Your first Guinness in Ireland. That's grand." She said.

"My first in Ireland. I have it regularly in America." He answered.

"Do you notice any difference in taste?" The other woman joined in.

"I think I do. Yes. Any way, I love the Guinness." He smiled.

"You're on holiday, then?" The second one asked.

"Yes. My first day."

"Your second day, really. You came in on Wednesday. Your plane was late."

Both women laughed.

Keane finished his sip.

"What? How did you know that?" He smiled back at them.

"I work at Shannon. I saw you at the bank. Margaret helped you. Then Brenda brought you to the bus stop."

"Well, so it is, then. My second day. Here's to my first day."

They all raised their pints and drank a sip.

"And now for your second day." The first woman said.

And again they all raised their glasses.

"How long are you staying?" The second woman asked Keane.

"I'll be here for most of the Summer. Six weeks. I'm staying in Kilshanny at Tullamore Farm House."

"Way up in Kilshanny? That's far in the country, I'd say." The publican interrupted.

"Hey, John, this guy's staying way out in the country."

She spoke to a gentleman smoking a long, curved ivory and mahogany pipe.

He was an older man with a gray beard and wavy gray hair.

"Kilshanny it is. She continued.

"What do you think of it?" She asked further.

"I'd hang me self." He spoke with a deep, gravelly, yet melodic, voice.

Everyone laughed at the gentleman's humor.

"That's a lovely place that Maeve and John have up there, though." The second woman spoke.

"Oh, I love it up there in the hills. It's so peaceful." Keane spoke.

"That peace'll be gettin' at ya after a spell, you know, if you don't watch yerself now."

The old man spoke again as he rose from his chair at the dark wood bar.

He held his long-curved pipe in his hand as he passed by Keane.

"Welcome to Ireland, son. Mind the peace now." And the old man left through the large wooden doors of Calvin's pub.

"You're staying on holiday for a nice stretch." The first woman spoke again.

"Yes, well, I have the time at the moment to do so."

"My name is Kathleen Cahill. This is my sister Ita Donohue." The first woman spoke again.

"My name is Patrick Keane. I'm very delighted to meet both of you. Thank you."

The pints were lifted, sipped, and placed down again on the dark wood bar. This activity carried on throughout the afternoon. The pints were lifted, sipped, and placed down again on the dark wood bar.

Between sips were laughs and conversation. It did not take the mixture of Guinness and time to forge an agreeable connection between the three souls laughing at the dark wood bar. The kindred seam was formed by an equitable friendliness inherent within each of them. Time and Guinness only added to the already existing congeniality.

And it was great fun for Keane. His loneliness was a lingering injury rooted in constant movement. He was always moving away. Whether it was the first move, the act of moving from a home, which coincidentally contained all the subsequent moves, or whether it was the continuous drift from within, Keane was always going away. He never allowed for the time to heal. The injury, the pain of the loneliness, persisted because he never became rooted in one place. And his soul was unsettled.

Keane sat sipping his pint of Guinness when Kathleen and Ita approached him.

"Patrick, we've made our phone call." Kathleen spoke to Keane.

"And guess what? We'd think it a lovely idea if you came along with us this evening. I've just called my husband to ask if it would be alright if you joined us. He was a bit nervous."

Kathleen laughed with that rolling pitch of sound. It is a sound filled with happiness.

"Patrick, you have to realize that Ita and myself don't ever sit in pubs picking up strangers." She continued, still laughing.

"But it would be grand if you joined us tonight. It'll be a hell of a night, Patrick. Mike, my husband, will be here about half eight. We're going to see a band that we know. Mark and Enda. Ita's man, Mark, sings in it. It's great fun. And we'll all get pissed." Her laugh rolled out with force.

"Say you'll join us and then we'll all have another pint to celebrate our meeting."

"I would love to join all of you. I've had a fantastic time this afternoon. Maybe it was too much fun as I've had quite a bit of Guinness. But I'd love to join you."

He looked at both of them and then back at Kathleen. He studied her face. She saw his look and took his hand.

"Grand!" And she let out with more laughter.

"I think I'll have a cigar." Keane spoke.

"Do they have cigars here?" He asked them.

"We have these short cigars in here. I don't know if that's what you would want." Ita told him.

The woman who served Keane the pint walked over, always hearing everything, and showed Patrick a short, black stub of a cigar.

"You could try the Aberdeen Arms Hotel across the street. I'm sure they have cigars." Kathleen pointed out.

"Oh, really? I think I'll walk over. If I don't fall over that is to say."

Keane rose from the chair and stood unsteadily for a moment.

"Easy boy. Go slow." Kathleen said jokingly.

Keane walked with a little unsteadiness as he left Galvin's for the hotel. The fresh air did him well.

He stepped into the Aberdeen Arms. After being shown some cigars in fine cases Keane chose one.

"Great. I'll take it. I can't believe I'll have a Cuban cigar."

He handed the young man a twenty pound note.

"Yes, sir."

"If you'll be needing any more please let me know. Thank you, sir." He handed back eight pounds.

"Thank you. Have a good evening." Keane said.

And he returned to Galvin's Pub.

"Now that's a cigar!" Kathleen shouted as Keane sat and presented the hand-rolled, Cuban cigar.

"Ha! Ha! It is at that, huh?" Keane laughed.

"It's a Cuban. I can't get these at home."

He lit the cigar and puffed on it lightly. The bluish-white smoke drifted slowly out of his mouth and lingered in a sweet-smelling cloud near his face.

"Boy, that tastes real good. Especially with a pint."

He lifted his tall pint glass and drank a good sip.

"Cheers!"

Both Kathleen and Ita were happy that Keane found a good cigar.

They all sat in the same chairs as at the beginning of the afternoon. Now Keane smoked his Cuban cigar and they spoke of music, the weather, and life in County Clare. But mostly it was about music. All three had a strong love for music.

"Anyone getting hungry? I'm starving." Keane asked.

"You don't want to eat here." Kathleen stated quietly as she shook her head slowly back and forth.

"No? Ok. Can you recommend a place?"

"I'd go to the Bayview or to The Shamrock Inn." Kathleen spoke to Keane.

"The Bayview is just next to the church next door, Patrick." Ita told Keane.

"Care to join me? I'm going to the Bayview. The least amount of walking right now the better."

"Patrick we've both eaten a big lunch. Why don't you walk over and we'll wait for you here. We'll try not to get too pissed while you're away." Kathleen let roll a laugh mixed with the words.

"I'm off."

Keane lifted himself off of the chair and grabbed his hat.

"Great hat, Patrick." Ita spoke.

"'tis a handsome hat. Unusual for around here." Kathleen said.

"I won't be gone too long. Just a quick something to eat. I can't keep up with you on the pints." He smiled.

"See you in just a bit."

He turned and stepped toward the large wooden doors of Calvin's Pub.

"Mind your step. Bye." Both said goodbye.

As the heavy wooden door swung its weight Keane felt the fresh air rush in mixing with the stale, unmoving air within the pub. As he stepped outside he realized how good it felt to be once again outdoors. It felt good to breathe the cooler air.

Keane did feel somewhat unsteady. It was a worthwhile effort to get something to eat. The night will soon begin which seemed to hint at the same activity as the afternoon.

Keane walked passed the church which sat uncomfortably next to Calvin's Pub. The grand structure of the church seemed oversized as it squeezed in between the row of narrow, low-lying buildings. Its immense shape cast a shadow over the street and footpath where Keane walked.

"Oh so you've returned have ye?" Kathleen commented.

"Yes. I'm back. John serves up a good meal at the Bayview."

He placing his hat on an empty stool.

"That's grand. You seem good and refreshed now." Ita said.

When the evening replaced the late afternoon, although unnoticeable, Keane and his new companions were still putting down pints.

"I've called Mike and he's on his way. It will be a moment before he is here." Kathleen announced as she returned from the public phone.

Keane was disappointed about missing the traditional music at Calvin's. But his disappointment was softened by the company of his new friends. The afternoon had been wonderful and refreshing for Keane. And the night was promising to be just as much fun.

"Are we all set then?" Kathleen, the leader, asked.

"Ready." Keane reported.

"Now." Ita spoke as she placed the empty pint glass down on the dark wood bar.

The three of them stepped out into the cool night air expectant with the promise of further excitement.

They were quiet for a moment taking in the fresh air of the night although still bright as day. The sun would not set until close to eleven o'clock during the Summer.

"Do you realize, Patrick, that we've been drinking damned near all day? I'd say we're all pissed right about now, sure."

Kathleen broke the silence and it moved away as the gaiety of the afternoon returned.

The three of them joked about drinking and the fun that took place inside Calvin's Pub. Just then a car pulled up with its horn blowing twice.

With the motor still running the driver jumped out and stepped around the car and joined the three on the footpath.

"Hello." He spoke in a. friendly, deep tone looking at Keane.

"What a day it's been, Mike. We're all pissed." Kathleen laughed loudly.

"And this is our new friend, Patrick Keane." She continued.

"Hello. Wonderful to meet you." Keane extended his hand as he spoke to Michael.

"Alright, same here. Welcome to Ireland."

He shook Keane's hand and with that everyone laughed from the excitement and the drink.

Mike and Kathleen jumped into the front seats after Ita and then Keane squeezed into the back seat of the small car.

"We're off, then." Mike said with a short laugh.

"We'll be hearing a good band tonight, Patrick. Very good music indeed." Mike continued.

"How was the day, Kathy?" Mike asked his wife.

"Oh grand. The craic was good. Patrick is lots of fun and I love Galvin's anyway." Kathleen spoke freely.

Kathleen did not seem to be bothered by any of life's trying moments.

The car started to sputter and shake as it tried to get going faster.

"C'mon now you." Mike spoke to the car.

"What kind of car is it, Mike?" Keane asked.

"It's a heap of shite is what it is." Mike answered loudly with a laugh.

Everyone laughed at the joke as the car started to quiet down and take the road more smoothly.

They drove along the coast road which traced Galway Bay. It was a twisting, winding road through the hills and pastures of County Clare. It was a long drive but Keane loved it as he looked out the window and watched as the car drove passed the bay on one side and the green hills on the other side. The mountains of Connemara rose in the misty background.

The time seemed to pass quickly as the conversation was lively and with the view framed by the window.

The car wound its way into a parking lot of a hotel and then stopped.

"Everyone out! We're here! Ballyvaughan!" Mike said with exaggeration.

The four of them bounced out of the car carrying the same excitement with which they left Lahinch.

They went through the door of the hotel and came upon a huge crowd.

They made their way to a table that Ita's friend, Mark, had saved for them. They gathered themselves at a small, round table sitting in the front. They sat while Mike stood and asked who was drinking.

"We're all drinking except you. We need a good driver. But you can have a pint now I suppose." Kathleen said.

Mike took the order which was all pints of Guinness. Keane asked to help with carrying them back to the table.

"Sit, sit, Pat." Mike motioned with his hand to Keane.

"Sit, Patrick. I'll go with Mike." Ita said.

Mark came over to the table after he finished setting up the equipment.

"Mark, hello." Kathleen said loudly and cheerfully. The noise in the room was very loud and thick with smoke.

"Good evening, Kate. How are you keeping?" Mark said.

"We've had a grand day. And we've picked up an American along the way. This is Patrick Keane." She looked at Mark and then at Keane.

"Patrick this is Mark."

Keane stood and shook Mark's hand.

"Happy to meet you, Mark." Keane said.

"It's a bit crowded and noisy in here, isn't it?" Mark said.

"Your band really packs them in." Keane spoke.

Mark sat and spoke with Kathleen and Keane until the other two came back carrying five pints.

Mark stood and helped place the pints down.

"Slanta, Patrick." Mark said as he placed the heavy, dark pint glass down in front of Keane.

"Cheers!" Keane said back to them all.

After a few minutes Mark got up and walked over to his place with the band.

When the band played Keane noticed the sound instantly. The room was vibrant with excitement. They were singing many American tunes.

The pints continued as they had during the afternoon hours.

"It's all just fun for us, Patrick. That's what it's all about for us." Kathleen said tellingly.

"And it looks like you are achieving it." He laughed.

The music and the pints went on. It was, in fact, a good time. Keane enjoyed it even though for him it was out of the ordinary. But he observed the fun more than he expressed it. He laughed, but studied them. He spoke, but listened more. As the night grew in hours and the band sang its last few songs Keane surrendered to the fun. The seriousness and the loneliness dissipated from his sheltered heart. The laughter was loud and the craic was good.

The four of them, Keane, Michael, Kathleen, and Ita piled back into Michael's car for the long, winding drive home. Michael had stopped after his two pints earlier on as Kathleen made him the designated driver.

"Pat, we'll go down this very narrow, steep, twisted, hill on our way home." Mike said.

"Oh that will be great fun. That's Corkscrew Hill, Patrick. I'm so pissed at the moment. I hope I don't get sick from it." Kathleen said.

After a few minutes they were on a very steep and narrow lane which twisted its way dangerously down.

"Here we go Patrick. Girls, hold on and don't get sick in my car." Mike was laughing out loud.

Everyone was screaming from the sharp turns and the quick spiraling downward motion of the narrow road.

"That's it. Fun's over. Let's go to Lahinch for some chips." Mike said as they continued on toward Lahinch.

It was very late now but a small eatery for take out was still operating. The four of them walked the skinny footpath eating their bags of fish and chips.

They walked the empty lot of O'Looney's that Keane had walked much earlier in the day, yesterday to be exact.

They stepped onto the sandy path and sat atop a stone wall above the crashing waves of high tide. The four of them sat in the blowing, shifting wind.

They ate fish and chips, laughed, and spoke of the things they did yesterday and through the night until the ocean met them.

"It's all for the fun of it, Patrick. Isn't it? We had such a grand time with you. The craic was brilliant."

Kathleen spoke into the blowing wind which carried her words over the sea.

The early morning hours drifted listlessly as the four of them walked the quiet, abandoned streets of Lahinch. Keane and his new friends wandered the night spending it freely as if no other day lie ahead.

When the hours were all spent and another day did indeed arrive it was time to go home. The evidence of the new day was witnessed in the faint morning light.

A few miles away from Lahinch Keane was back in the hills of Kilshanny. Mike's car sputtered up the long farmhouse drive to the top where Tullamore sat restful under the dome of the sparsely lit morning sky.

Keane stood in the early morning breeze wearing his Akubra watched the car roll down the long farmhouse drive.

He felt better now that he was back on the hill. Back at home, almost.

Keane quietly entered through the front door and walked to his room.

He removed his smoke-filled clothes and discarded them into a large bag he kept in the standing closet. He put on a pair of shorts and grabbed everything he would need for a shower. He left his room and walked down the hall.

He changed, not for bed, but to go out. He put on a pair of khaki shorts and a tee-shirt with a sweater over it. He grabbed his Akubra, thick with the smell of cigarettes, and left his room.

He started down the farmhouse road. He walked in the airy, morning light. The hidden sun shed its rays on wet hues of green. This stretch of narrow, bony road sliced through more pastures and more hills. Keane stopped to watch the sheep that were grazing. It was a beautiful sight in which to watch and be a part.

He continued on the winding road. He stretched his legs enough to feel the evening leave his body and spirit. He renewed them both in these rising and falling green hills.

As Keane walked up a steep hill the road bent in a new direction and Keane saw the glimmer of the climbing, white spire in the distance. It rose above the soft, wet hue of green layered beneath its tall, slim structure. Keane stopped to admire that view, and to respect it.

He entered the Catholic Kilshanny church freely. He sat in the back pew and rested. And then he prayed. He rose from kneeling and walked out of the church.

Standing outside of the wrought iron gate he once again peered at the church. Keane turned and headed back the same way in which he had just walked. After a while he saw Tullamore, great and stately, sitting on the hill which lifted the home high above all the hills.

8

Into This Land

Her knock came as softly as breath upon a cheek. Pauline was just that way. She was soft, quiet, and gentle. So her knock for Keane was the first gentle breeze of the day. And although tired, he awoke quickly to answer that tender, quiet rhythm.

"Good morning. Breakfast is ready now, Patrick."

Pauline smiled as she looked down and away.

"Good morning, Pauline." Keane touched her hands which were folded in front of her.

"I'm so happy to see you this morning." Keane said.

Pauline looked up at Keane and gave her smile fully to him.

"Did you have a good time in Lahinch?" She asked quietly.

"Oh, what a night. I met some people in town and I only arrived home a short time ago."

"Grand. I'd love to hear about it." She said as she gripped his hand and moved him toward the dining room.

At the table Pauline brought Patrick a cup of coffee.

"I've decided you wanted coffee this morning. Since you've come in awfully late this morning I thought this would be best."

Pauline placed the hot, steaming cup of coffee in front of Keane.

"Now,"

"Ah, Pauline, Yes, coffee. You've guessed correctly. I came in at just after five o'clock."

Keane picked up the coffee cup and put it to his lips and sipped.

"Oh my, Patrick, it must have been a very grand evening indeed." Pauline said as she stood by his side.

"I started in Lahinch as you know. And there I met Kathleen Cahill and her sister Ita Donohue. From there they invited me to Ballyvaughan to hear Mark and Enda in their band." Keane said as he sipped more of his coffee.

"Grand. I know Mark and Enda. They're quite good. Actually I know the girls, too." Pauline said with interest.

"It was a great night. When I came back I changed and took a walk to the church. Absolutely beautiful! I can't get over the beauty that is around me. And even in front of me. You never know where you may encounter it."

Pauline blushed and reached to straighten the linen cloth that was neat and fine on the table.

"Lovely. You must be awfully tired now, though, Patrick. Will you rest this morning?"

"I think I'll go to the hills, Pauline, To the hills." Patrick said in a laughing tone.

He had become very comfortable with Pauline now. He felt very good about having someone near with whom he could be himself. He very much enjoyed Pauline's company.

"Would you be in Ennistymon again today, Patrick?" Pauline asked tentatively.

Keane gave her a quick side glance.

"If you'll have tea with me again, I'd love to go to Ennistymon."

"I noticed a narrow, dirt road on my way back from the church. It cut through the pastures and went straight up a long, steep hill. I think I'll see about it."

"Oh yes. I'm often on that lane. I live up around that area."

"Oh, ok. Well, you'll probably see me often then as I walk past. Of course, you'll get sick of me by then." Keane laughed.

"No. I won't mind at'tall. I hope I see you today." Pauline stated in her quiet tone.

The quiet was broken by a voice from the kitchen.

"Pauline? Pauline?" Maeve shouted from the kitchen. Her voice booming with command as it shattered the morning.

"Pauline!"

Maeve found Pauline speaking with Keane at his breakfast table.

"Pauline!" She said in a quieter tone.

"Bring the poor man his breakfast. You're not goin' to marry the man now so early in the mornin' are ye?"

Maeve had no problem stating things as she saw them.

"After all, Mr. Patrick Keane from America had an early rise this mornin', didn't he?" She looked at Keane with that crooked broad smile of hers that she used for just such occasions.

"Patrick. That shower sounds like cannons at five- ten in the morning. I'm afraid my room is just above and it is an awful noise from up there. Perhaps, if it is fine with you, can you take your showers after seven in the mornin'?"

"Of course of course, that is no bother to me. I should've realized about the noise."

He was about to stand.

"Sit, sit. And enjoy your coffee. Now, Pauline will bring out your breakfast. You had a late night, Patrick." She laughed.

"John and I were worried about you."

Although Maeve laughed she was indeed concerned for his well-being.

"I met Kathleen Cahill and her sister Ita Donohue in Calvin's Pub. We had a great time. Then they invited me out with Kathleen's husband, Mike, to Ballyvaughan to listen to Mark and Enda."

"Yes I know the Donohue girls. Very, very nice girls. They love their fun, don't they now? And Mark and Enda do a lovely job with the songs. I've heard them before myself in Lisdoonvarna."

Maeve had a knowledge of everything around her. From her position on the highest hill it seemed she saw it all.

"Yes, so I came in at about five this morning." Keane said.

"Yes I know, Patrick. But I'm glad you met some fine people and had a lovely time. Grand!"

Of course Maeve knew what time he came in.

"I'll be having more guests today, Patrick. The other two, the couple from England, will be leaving this morning. Another couple from England will be joining us today. His wife is from Dublin. They sound very nice, Patrick."

She didn't have to give him that information. But she did.

Pauline brought Keane his breakfast. She worked nervously in front of Maeve who watched her every move.

"Now, mind the plate. It's hot, Patrick." Pauline said quietly.

She turned abruptly and went back into the kitchen to finish her chores.

"Enjoy your breakfast, Patrick. We'll speak afterwards." Maeve said and turned toward the kitchen.

"Pauline?" She once again boomed out Pauline's name like cannon fire as she went through the kitchen doors.

Keane laughed to himself and began eating his breakfast. He thought about the day that lies ahead. He was tired but he needed to walk and see where it would bring him.

Back in his room he pulled the wicker chair from the corner to the window and sat. He reached for his Hebrew bible and opened to the Psalms. He read in ancient Hebrew the words that were put down so many centuries ago.

As he read he peered out the window. In the far distance down the slopes of green aiming high was the narrow spire of the church.

Keane thought about the previous night as he held the Psalms and peered out the window. It was immense fun. But as he sat in the wicker chair looking out onto the green hills he juxtaposed the night with the morning. He thought of the fun but thought also of the walk this morning. It brought him great peace to walk that narrow, bony road.

"It's all just fun for us, Patrick."

Keane thought of Kathleen's words.

It needed to be more than fun for Keane.

He read the Psalms looking for the answer. Every few lines he would look up from the ancient text and study the view out of his window.

After some meditation Keane laid down on the single bed that was covered with the two gray-patterned woolen blankets. He lay down with his arms folded under his head and his legs stretched out and crossed. He stared out the window as he lay atop the bed. Eventually he was lulled to sleep by the peace, the view, and having only had a few hours sleep previous.

He awoke about an hour later and stood at the sink that was near the standing closet. He dropped his hands down into the running water and lifted them to his face. He splashed his eyes and all around his face with the cool water. He still felt drowsy from the lack of sleep and the fatigue that drains the person after consuming too many pints.

Keane met Maeve in the hall on his way out. Maeve and John cleaned the home each morning when the guests went out for the day.

"Going out, Patrick?" Maeve asked.

"Yes. I'm going for a walk. I love the hills all around."

"Good morning, Mr. O'Connor." Keane added as he noticed John coming through the glass and wood French doors of the dining room. He was carrying a bucket of cleaning materials.

"Good mornin' to you." John answered politely.

He was a quiet farmer. He was connected to all of this land all of his life.

"Now you'll be callin' him John. No formalities here, Patrick." Maeve interrupted.

"Fine, Maeve. Thank you. I don't know how long I'll be gone. A few hours maybe and then off to Ennistymon for lunch."

"Grand. Have fun with Pauline. Take your time with the day, Patrick. Enjoy yourself. It's lovely land out there. And the sun is cooperating with us for once." She smiled.

Pauline was carrying more bedding as Keane met her on his way out.

"Hello Pauline. I'm going out walking."

"Grand. You must be tired, though. Patrick." She said to him while holding the bedding in her frail arms.

"I am at that. But, it was worth the fun. I'll hike the hills for a while and then go to Ennistymon for lunch with you. If you still like."

"It'd be lovely if you came for a visit."

"Pauline."

He stopped.

"Yes, Patrick?"

She put the bedding down.

"Last night was great fun. I really did have a fine time. But truthfully, having lunch with you yesterday was so much more meaningful. I would trade a thousand nights like last night for just one more lunch with you."

He peered into her eyes for an answer, gripping her soul with his vision.

"Patrick, that was lovely of you to say."

She stood a moment longer wanting to reach for his hand.

"I just wanted you to know. I'm looking forward to seeing you today."

He reached for her hand and held it just for a moment.

Keane didn't go far before he came upon the narrow dirt road. He walked feeling the bare earth under him. To be this close, this connected, to the earth filled Keane with a sense of wonder and belonging.

The narrow, dirt road climbed steadily. Tullamore was in view on its high perch atop Kilshanny. This road went high and steep and Keane was stretching his legs to meet the demand. It was almost as if he was walking through the pastures as the overgrowth spilled onto the edges of the unpaved road.

At the top of the narrow, dirt road stood two homes on either side and one with a large barn nearest the road. Two dogs wandered near the barn. The clamor of metal and voices poked out into the peaceful morning.

Tullamore was still visible as Keane continued his walk.

Soon the road began its descent. And the drop was sudden. Keane seemed to be almost looking straight down to the valley below. He touched the brim of his Akubra and lifted it slightly.

In the valley the walk seemed to go on forever. Keane blended into the pastures which surrounded him. He was alone in the splendor of the land. The ethereal cast of colors spread under and beyond Keane as he seemed to be lifted above the pastures in all their wonder. The dome of blue above him, so close to the earth he walked on, seemed to hold him down keeping him from ascending.

And he walked on. He walked on through the pastures present, through the pastures past, and as he walked his own past seemed to fall from him. His life was transforming as he stepped into the mystic. Remnants of his life were being discarded on the narrow, dirt road. The fragments of his life that Keane could not before discard, could not before let go, he abandoned now, on this narrow, dirt road.

The construct of a past seemed more worthwhile than the construct of emptiness. But neither was real. These were fragments clinging to Keane much the same as the craters clung to the dirt road.

Keane could feel truth upon his soul. Truth appears when the illusive shadows are shed from the coming light. And Keane's life had been illusory.

He walked on. The narrow, dirt road rose again and the dome of the sky lowered. The straightness of the road stopped and Keane turned onto a paved road.

On both sides of the narrow, bony road grew high hedges. Keane couldn't tell what was beyond them. He guessed it was more of the same pastures. On the one side had to be pastures since he was just walking through a part of them on the narrow, dirt road.

It went on like this for a lengthy part of the walk. Suddenly the hedges dropped away and the pastures quickly appeared as they stretched out far across the valley. They rose wondrously in all their hues of green atop the hills.

The suddenness of their appearing was so dramatic that they seemed to pull Keane in their direction. He stood and looked at the incredible display of beauty before him.

For a few moments Keane had thought that he was high above them and that the valley was far below him. It did appear that way due to the shades of green and the distance in which the quilt of pastures spread. It was a wonderful illusion. Once the view was studied it became visible that the valley and the bony road were on one and the same level.

Keane laughed at the thought of his mistake of thinking something was distant when it was in fact so near. He walked on.

Soon he came upon an opening that was most likely used by the tractors and for moving the herds to new grazing land. There was a long metal cross gate stretched across the opening hinged on two huge stone walls on either side.

Keane sat down on one stone wall and peered out into the land seeking it with his soul.

He reached back into his pocket and took out the tin whistle he had carried with him. He tooted on it once or twice and then played a series of notes. The scale of 'D' rang out through the valley. One long note was interrupted a few times by shorter notes, grace notes, to gather the sound of the whistle.

He played the Irish airs that he always enjoyed. The music floated mystically over the green pastures. The sound reached the farthest hills and came back with a deeper, truer sound having shed the initial impact of the notes. The air floated back as natural as the daylight. It was a fitting moment. The view and the land and being so close to home inspired him.

Keane played to the morning, he played to the day. He sat alone atop a white-washed stone wall. He was nearly home. And he felt it to his bones.

"That's a lovely tune."

Her voice was as gentle as the sloping hills with their soft green blanket.

"Pauline?"

Keane turned around with a rapid movement and jumped off of the wall.

"You play the whistle very well, very lovely." Pauline said quietly.

"Thank you very much." He spoke slowly.

"I hope it wasn't too corny to play such a thing as I sit near a green Irish pasture."

"Not at'tall, Patrick. Ireland is music."

"Do you like the traditional music?"

"I do, yes. I used to dance the traditional step dancing."

"Did you? I'd love to see you sometime. Now, you're out of Maeve's early, right?"

"Yes. Not too many guests so I'm able to leave earlier than other days."

"I think I'll come here often. This is so very beautiful." He turned slightly and swept his hand across the sky.

"I just live up the way a bit. I pass here quite often. I'll see you here again. Take care, Patrick. Keep well. I must be going home. I'm due at Foley's soon. Bye." She smiled and waved her hand in a slow motion.

"Bye, Pauline. See you in town soon."

"I was hoping for it." She smiled at him. Her long, dark red hair blew gently in the breeze.

And she walked on until the hedges covered her shape.

Maeve stepped briskly which is her fashion and pulled open the front door.

"Hello!" Maeve said with a broad smile.

"And welcome to Tullamore!" She continued.

"How are ye?"

The couple stepped into the front room of Tullamore.

"You must be Maeve." The gentleman spoke.

"I'm Paul Martin. This is my wife, Kay." Paul spoke in a confident, friendly manner.

"Come in and have a seat."

Maeve brought Paul and Kay to the two seats against the far window.

"Shall I make tea, then? You must be needing it after your long drive."

"Perfect. Tea would be lovely, Maeve." Paul spoke in clear English tones.

"I have one guest now. An American. A very lovely gentleman. He traveled alone. He came by bus to Ennistymon. He doesn't care to drive." Maeve explained.

They all sat in the front sitting room with the mural-like windows portraying the sweeping view of green hills.

"Sounds charming, Maeve." Paul said and sipped his tea.

"What location, Maeve, do I spot down that way?" Paul was pointing as he spoke.

"It looks quite lovely by the sea." He continued.

"That would be Lahinch. A seaside resort with some fine shops and restaurants and the pubs are many as well."

"Could you recommend a spot in which to get a bite to eat? I'm rather famished at the moment. Kay?" Paul asked.

"Yes, I feel a bit famished myself." Kay answered.

"Of course. Grand. Now. Here are some brochures of the places in town. And at your leisure please come and look at all the brochures I have of the surrounding areas. Please ask me any thing you need to know. Now. As for a restaurant. I'll recommend The Bayview. John is a lovely man. He's the proprietor. Fine food, lovely place."

"Wonderful, Maeve. Thank you very much. You've certainly been a big help. Perhaps later in the day we'll run in to you again?" He asked.

"Perhaps." She nodded and continued.

"But just in case what time would you like your breakfast? The American has his breakfast at half-eight. But, of course, you are welcome to choose any time you would like."

"Kay? What would be your preference? For myself, it would make no difference."

"Half-eight would be lovely. This way we could get an early start for Galway." Kay looked at her husband and then Maeve.

"Lovely. Would you be going to Galway in the morning?"

"We're not sure, Maeve." Paul spoke.

"We're going to see how the day fairs and how we feel in the morning."

"Grand. Have a wonderful day."

Before she disappeared through the dining room for the final time she gave them directions to Lahinch.

Keane was stretched out on the flat whitewashed stone wall. His Akubra was lying on his stomach. His arms were folded behind his head. The whistle leaned against the inside of his hat shining in the sunlight.

He awoke gradually leaning forward and slightly upward. Slowly he sat upright with his legs dangling off of the edge of the old wall. He rubbed both hands on his face. He then remembered that he must visit Pauline. He didn't want the day to go on without seeing her.

He hopped off of the stone wall, stretched, grabbed his hat from the flat surface of the rock and started his walk.

Pauline was helping someone in the shop when the high-pitched bell rang. Keane walked in and waited until she was finished.

"It's been very busy today, Patrick." "But I'm so glad you're here. How are you keeping?" "I'm well, thanks. Do you have time for lunch?" "I think I can manage to leave now. John-Joe is in the back. He'll close up shop."

They went to the Archway Pub for a small meal and a pint. The pub was located near a brick and stone archway that arched over a narrow side street. The river was in view from within the Archway Pub. It was a quiet place.

Pauline and Keane sat at a table in the small, glass-enclosed patio of the pub.

"You must be so tired, Patrick. Maybe you should've stayed back and slept more."

"I wanted to come and see you. I'm having a wonderful time.

"I think I will sleep later, though." He laughed.

"It was very kind of you to come for a visit. It's quite a long walk, Patrick."

It was a quiet time. The two of them did not need many words. They felt at ease in the silence. Afterward they walked the narrow footpath of the main street. They strolled leisurely passed the small shops that decorated the street. They went in some of the shops to have a look. They laughed at some things and Keane made her laugh by acting silly at times.

Pauline enjoyed Keane's company. He made her laugh and he made her think. He made her feel things, too. She was as alone as he.

Paddy took them back to Kilshanny. He dropped Keane off at the white-stone and wood bridge.

The long farmhouse road was even longer uphill. Keane stretched his legs and his lungs to meet this demanding incline. At the top he saw the tall tree spreading its thick nest of branches over the front pasture that lay at

Tullamore's doorstep. And there was Tullamore glimmering in the afternoon sun.

Maeve was cleaning the long, open area of the front room. Pushing in chairs after 'using the Hoover' as she liked to say. She had already cleaned the windows. She had opened the front door to put a plant outside on the wood ledge when she saw Patrick Keane walking up the drive. She giggled half aloud at the hat he was wearing. She didn't mind it, though, and thought it was a handsome piece, but just a bit out of place in Kilshanny.

Everyone came here with cars, she thought. And there he is walking everywhere he goes. But he's a polite man and someone nice with whom to speak. She peered at him as he climbed the long, steep drive. Then she turned and went back inside to continue her chores.

Maeve did the last few things to have the sitting room in order for her guests before she disappeared through the dining room door. She stopped inside the dining room and surveyed the tables. Yes, she thought, everything seems right at the moment. She stepped briskly into her kitchen. She closed the door behind her. John was sitting in his favorite chair with the television turned on listening to the news in part to get updates on the sports.

John O'Connor had a white mop of hair on his head. He was a thin man who moved slowly but with strong movements. This time of day, if there were no problems on the farm and there could be many at any time, found John in that very chair with the television on.

It was his land. It came from his people. It had been generations handed to generations of his people that kept this land. He knew no other place. He was a Clare man through and through. The O'Connors were numerous in County Clare.

Time and again John could be seen walking the green slopes of the pastures that drooped downward and outward from his home atop all the hills. This was besides the time he could be seen working on the hills moving cattle or running the tractor, and checking the ground for mildew after one of the many rains. The other times he just walked the land with his stick at his side. He didn't use the stick for anything but to carry now and again.

He was a man of over sixty. The land would go to his son and daughter. The land is a hard place he told them both. The land is a hard place.

Maeve opened the Bed & Breakfast some fifteen years ago when times seemed to get harder and the land with the cows and sheep was not turning things in their favor. They took their savings and mortgaged their land, the land that John was given to oversee, the land that had been with his family and name for well over a century, and the land that was in his blood.

They did renovations on the home to accommodate the people Maeve had hoped would come. It turned out well for John and Maeve O'Conner. The people did come.

The land was still worked as a farm and Maeve, with her insight, ran the Bed & Breakfast. This set them up comfortably. It could have gotten much worse than the inconveniences of smaller private quarters for the family since the rest of the house was needed for guests.

Maeve opened the B & B from March through September. Sometimes through early October it remained opened. It depended on when the Lisdoonvarna festival fell on the calendar. It was a trying business, though.

"More guests should be arriving soon, John." Maeve said as she closed the door.

"But for now, we're safe." They both laughed.

"I see that Patrick Keane, the American, is coming in from his walk. He doesn't want to drive, John."

She looked at her husband waiting for an explanation.

"I don't know, dear. Maybe he's from the city and doesn't drive. Maybe he'll get himself a car later on. We'll see." He was sipping a cup of tea.

"He's a nice man, though. Very polite. I hope he'll do well staying here. It's such a long time. Isn't it, dear?"

"'tis unusual for what we're used to havin'. I'd say he'll be alright. Seems to love the land. That's important." John said as he stretched his long legs out.

"Well, he paid all in advance. We'll need that money saved, please God. And he didn't use any of those terrible vouchers, thank you."

"We've been saved by the sun, dear. No rain for a few days now. Won't last, though." John murmured the last few words.

He despised the word rain. The last half a dozen years or so Ireland had been deluged by the rain. The pattern persisted with much damage.

"More tea, John?" Maeve asked as she carried a plate of biscuits and scones over to her husband.

John sat comfortably near the wood-burning stove which also had a stove top attachment. This was a sitting room for the family. It was a small, compact room with a couch along the window edge and John's chair near the wood-burning stove. The television was against the opposite wall. In the off-season Maeve opened up the dining room once again as the family sitting room. But for now this was their private place. And it was very comfortable for the family. Mark, their son, did not spend much time in the sitting room. Their daughter, Kathleen, lived in Dublin. John and Maeve spent comfortable moments watching television or listening to the radio. They both loved music.

The morning came again with its clear skies. Keane awoke early and climbed out of the woolen blankets. He washed up at the sink and moved the wicker chair to the window ledge. Facing out toward the hills Keane went to the ancient Psalms. He loved the mornings. And this seemed such a perfect place to open the ancient texts and look out on the ancient land.

When seven o'clock came around Keane went down the hall to shower. Afterwards he dressed in shorts and sweater, put on his Clark shoes, grabbed his Akubra and stepped out of his room.

He walked down the long, winding farmhouse road. The sun was beginning to peak over the hills making them shine from the morning dew. He made the turn at the bottom over the white-stone and wood bridge. The sheep were there grazing and again one sheep saw Keane and alerted the rest and they all went to the same corner huddling by the old white-washed stone walls.

It was cool for a summer's morning. And the pastures still rose and fell in a gentle, peaceful manner.

Soon he saw the white, narrow spire of the church. When the sun hit it directly it shone brilliantly against the hues of green.

He stood at the wrought-iron black fence. After standing for some moments he pulled the gate open and went in. The Catholic church was open and welcoming.

Keane went in the back pew again. He knelt and prayed.

"Have you come home?"

Keane heard the voice as he knelt.

He was startled not by the voice but by the question. He looked up from his prayer.

"Good morning, Father." Keane rose as he spoke.

"I very, very rarely see any at'tall in here this time of day. And when I do it is usually someone who has come home to the church. What brought them here I do not know but I know they've come home. That has been my experience."

"It's good to see some one here and I'm not all alone. My name is Father Kelly."

Later in the day when Keane met John sitting in the front room he told him about meeting the priest.

"I've met Father Kelly this morning at the church."

"Oh yes. He's a Galway man."

John identified people by way of their region. And Father Kelly's people, as well as Father Kelly himself, are Galway people.

"Hello Father Kelly. I'm Patrick Keane."

"From America." Father Kelly stated.

"Welcome to Ireland. I hope to see you again at Mass." Father Kelly said kindly.

He studied Keane looking for the reason Reane may be here at this hour praying.

"Yes, you will, Father."

"Keep well, God bless." Father Kelly put his hand momentarily on Keane's shoulder.

The gentle knock of Pauline, like an angel on a soul, came softly as Keane sat in the wicker chair facing out toward the surrounding hills.

"Good morning, Patrick. Breakfast is up." She smiled and stayed a moment.

Keane took her smile into his heart.

"Good morning. I'm ready."

"I had a fine time with you yesterday. Did you sleep well?"

"I did, yes. And I've had my walk to the church already. I met Father Kelly."

"He's a lovely man."

They moved to the dining room.

"I'll get your coffee, then?" Pauline knew he did but asked anyway.

"Great, some coffee. Thanks."

He sat at the familiar table. The room was empty. He did hear two people speaking from upstairs. He wondered if they would be at breakfast.

"Now." Pauline placed the hot, steaming cup of coffee in front of Patrick.

"Maeve's getting your food ready. It'll be out in a moment."

"I'm well rested, Pauline. Last night I had a very exciting night. I stayed in my room and slept. Well, I did do a little reading. But nothing as far as going out to Lahinch or Ennistymon."

"No pints, then? Well, you have today to catch up." She smiled again.

"What will you do today? The sun is cooperating. Will you be at the wall today? Perhaps playing your whistle?"

"I think I will go there. I loved it so very much. After that, well, I'm not sure. Maybe walk to Ennistymon. Will you be very busy today?"

"Oh, do stop in. That would be lovely. If I'm busy, I'll manage a break or you can stay a while and we can chat. If you have the mind to stay."

"I will. I'll walk down today and visit. I would love that very much. What time would you be arriving at Foley's?"

"I should be there by half-twelve. It's slow at the B & B so I will be leaving here early. Well, then. I'll see you in town."

"Pauline?" Maeve again.

Pauline never seemed to be where Maeve wanted her at any given moment.

"Ah, your breakfast is up." Pauline spun quickly and darted into the kitchen.

Pauline came out carrying the large, hot plate of food. She placed it down in front of Keane.

"Now. Mind the plate. It's hot." She stepped away a short distance.

"Thank you, Pauline." He lifted his fork and knife.

"Enjoy your breakfast. I'll see you in town." She spoke softly.

"I'll probably see you before I go for my walk." He said and started to eat his breakfast.

"Grand." And she left through the kitchen doors.

Keane finished his breakfast and pushed his chair back away from the table, stood and went to his room.

As he was walking toward the front door Pauline passed him.

"Have a good walk." She told him.

"Yes, it's another beautiful morning. Almost finished?" He asked her.

"Not quite. I've got to ready another room. More guests coming today. And the two here now haven't eaten yet. So I've got some time to spend here yet. So I'll see you in town today?"

That smile came across her face like light brushing away a shadow.

"Yes. I'll be there about the time you should be showing up at Foley's."

"That'll be grand. See you then, Patrick."

"Yes. Uh-oh, I think Maeve's about to call you again. Bye." They both laughed.

Keane looked up at the narrow, dirt road. He started his uphill climb and watched as Tullamore rose with him as he walked near its height. Soon he disappeared passed the barn with the same two dogs in front and the same clamor of metal and voices from within the large barn. Then the downward slope clutched at his steps with its steepness. But the beauty of it grabbed at his soul. The convergence of the narrow, dirt road sloping steeply down and then dipping as the green pastures rose gave the illusion of walking momentarily above them. This only added to the mystical aura which Keane was already experiencing.

Keane walked the rise and fall of the narrow, dirt road to the place he had found the previous morning.

He found his place on the flat, stone wall. He looked out at it again. He took his whistle out and played his air. The slow, melodic sound floated across the pastures.

Later when Keane stood at the highest of the three peaks on the narrow, bony road to Ennistymon he looked out toward the direction of his new-found place. He wondered if the sound of the whistle could still be heard as it floated across the hues of green. He didn't really think so. Music exists in time. But, then again, Keane thought, these hills are timeless.

He stood on that high peak and looked out toward Tullamore. Beyond there, he thought, is that place. He loved sitting on that stone wall and playing the whistle or just looking out onto the far reaches of the pastures in all their rise and fall.

He found Pauline sitting again in the cold, damp back room of Foley's.

"Back at the potatoes, huh?" He laughed.

"Oh, hi Patrick. It's lovely that you've dropped in."

She continued with the potatoes. The sound of the motor was loud as it roared to peel the potatoes.

"Would you like a cup of tea?" She asked.

"No. I'm fine, thanks."

"Did you go to your place and play your whistle?"

"Yes, I did. I'll never get over the beauty of the place."

"I just have this bunch of potatoes to get ready for delivery to the hotel in Lahinch and then I'm off. There's not much today. It's kind of slow." Pauline looked at Keane.

"Oh, great! That means we can go get something to eat. Would that be fine with you or, do you have somewhere to go?"

"No, I'm free." She smiled at him.

Both of them walked down the narrow footpath of Ennistymon. Pauline was explaining where everything was located in town. She became very animated as she spoke. Keane saw the child in her and he smiled while she spoke.

"We can go to O'Neil's for lunch. They'll be serving chicken nuggets and chips today."

"That sounds American."

"It probably is American."

"Let's go, then." He said.

The two of them, both free, set off down the narrow footpaths of Ennistymon. Pauline was looking after Keane.

Afterward Pauline and Keane walked along the river. They climbed the high stone wall and walked along its flattened ledge. The river pushed by them.

The wind blew and Keane removed his hat. That was the only sound, the wind blowing through the tiny space between them. Keane turned on the ledge and faced Pauline. She came to a sudden stop and landed in Keane's arms.

His hands grasped her arms. He peered into her deep, dark eyes. She stood as still as the earth beneath her. The river pushed by them. The wind was steady. Their hearts were pumping with wonder and mystery. A moment could be like that.

The wind released them and Keane dropped his hands from her arms which remained frozen in midair.

They walked back to the main street.

"Oh, this is where you live. I've passed this a few times already." Keane said as he got out of Paddy's car to say good-bye to Pauline.

"Yes, this is it. Would you like to come in, Patrick?"

"Thank you, Pauline. I would love to come in."

Patrick Keane entered Pauline's world in the hills of Kilshanny. She held the door for him as he entered her home. She directed him to the living room.

"I'll make some tea, then." She went into the kitchen.

Keane got up from his seat and looked at the music collection. He took one compact disc out and held it.

"I love this song, Pauline." He shouted to her.

"Please feel free to put it on, Patrick."

The sound of Ritchie Havens' *Follow' came out and filled the room.

Pauline stood at the entrance to the living room and hummed the tune.

"I love this song. I can't find many who do." She continued to hum the song.

"Oh I've loved it for a long, long time now. I can't believe such an unknown record is here in Kilshanny."

Pauline carried the tea out and placed the cups and pot on a table near the couch.

They drank their tea and played the tune over a few times.

The emptiness of their lives drained and was replaced by the warmth of belonging. Keane looked into Pauline's eyes and she looked into his eyes. In another moment their eyes shifted and their faces were frozen in that instant. Their expressions were framed by the window which showed the hills of Kilshanny.

The day slowly drifted as Patrick Keane was entertained by the company of Pauline O'Sullivan. After much time Keane mentioned going back to Tullamore.

"Perhaps I'll get cleaned up from all my walking. Would you like to get together in a little while?"

Pauline smiled broadly.

"Yes! Of course. I'll be here. Just come over or call if you like."

"You had a phone call, Patrick." Maeve came out to tell Keane. She heard him come in.

"It was Kathleen Cahill." She told Keane.

"Oh, I'm sorry I missed the call." Keane said sounding somewhat preoccupied.

"She will call back shortly. I wasn't sure where you were." She stood waiting in case Keane came forth with any news.

He did.

"I was out in the hills for a while. Then I walked again to Ennistymon." He gave her his news.

"Lunch again with Pauline?" She smiled.

"Oh, uh, yes. It was a good time." He said nervously.

"That's quite a walk you managed, Patrick."

Maeve changed the subject perceiving Keane's discomfort.

"I love that walk. There is so much beauty to see. It goes on and on. I'll probably do that walk many times."

"If the weather cooperates as it has been." She said in a sterner tone wary of the rain that must come.

Maeve came to Keane's room a short while later. He was resting on the single bed.

"Patrick! Patrick?" She didn't just knock as Pauline would have done.

"Patrick?" She didn't give him much time to get off of the bed and answer the door.

"Yes, coming." He jumped off of the bed and swung the door open.

"Patrick, you have a phone call. Kathleen has rung again."

She put her hand on his shoulder to guide him more quickly to the phone.

Keane laughed at the way Maeve would rush.

She handed Patrick the phone.

"Hello?"

"Hello, Patrick. It's Kathleen Cahill. I hope your keeping well. Any news?" She asked with that natural vibrancy of her personality.

"Hi Kathleen. No, no news. I'm just resting at the moment. I did some miles of walking today."

"Listen, Patrick. Mike and I and Ita will be meeting at the Shamrock Inn at about half-nine. It'd be lovely if you join us. Mark and Enda will be playing there tonight."

"That sounds wonderful. I'll be there a little bit before that for something to eat. I'll save us a table."

Then Keane thought of something.

"Listen, Kathleen, would it be fine with you if I bring Pauline O'Sullivan?"

"Oh grand. She's lovely. We'll all have fun. The place will get full rather quickly. So, it's set. We'll see you tonight, Patrick."

"Yes. Thank you. See you tonight." He hung up the phone.

Maeve laughed.

"They'll keep you out 'till sunrise again, Patrick. Mind yourself now."

She laughed and the laugh gently settled into a smile.

"And don't keep Pauline out too late now. She must work in the morning, Patrick Keane!"

"Oh I hope I don't stay out all night again. That's too much for me."

"But I do enjoy their company." He continued.

Lying on the bed he stared out the large window. The tall trees swayed in the wind that came off of the ocean a few miles away. Things were working out, he thought. He has met some very kind people. The B & B that he chose could not be a better one and certainly Maeve and John were very caring folk. Kathleen and Mike and Ita provided the fun. And then there was Pauline. Things were working out fine and much better than he could have imagined, he thought. He felt at peace. The trees were swaying in a huddled movement.

He saw Maeve walk out into their midst. She went through their middle to where she hung her laundry. She came out in full view again standing with the trees. She stood against the wind as the trees moved.

He went in and asked Maeve to phone Gerry Hartigan for a lift to Lahinch.

Gerry came a short time later.

"Hello Patrick! goin' to Lahinch are ye?" He said in his full voice.

"Yes. But first I'll be going to pick up Pauline O'Sullivan."

"Ah, sure. I know the house. We'll swing over to get her then."

The Shamrock Inn was nestled in the middle of the low sitting buildings on the main street in Lahinch. It was half a block away from Galvin's Pub. On the ground floor there were two restaurants. One was for formal dining and the other, near the bar, was for casual gatherings. Keane chose the informal setting. This would be where the band would play.

It was dark in the Shamrock Inn. The Bayview was lit by plenty of window light. The Shamrock Inn preferred the dark and private atmosphere.

"Hello Patrick." It was Michael. And behind him were Kathleen and Ita.

"Hello Michael. Hi Kathleen. Hello Ita." He stood to greet them.

"This is Pauline O'Sullivan of Kilshanny."

"Hello Pauline!" Mike said.

"Pauline, glad you've joined us." Kathleen said.

Kathleen and Ita already knew Pauline.

"Hi Pauline. I haven't seen you for some time now." Ita said.

"Yes, 'tis been a while indeed. I'm looking forward to tonight. Thank you." She said, always gracious.

"I hope this table is fine with you." Keane said to all of them.

"It's grand, Patrick. Thanks for getting here early to reserve it." Ita spoke.

Ita was the taller and more narrow of the two sisters. She was an artist. And she spoke as one, too.

Her words were chosen carefully. Unlike Kathleen, with red hair all the way down her back, who spoke with the freedom of not caring how she sounded.

A round of pints were brought to the table by Michael. Kathleen, Ita, Pauline and Patrick reached for a pint. Michael sat down.

"Good spot right by the bar, Patrick. Good thinking." Mike said with a laugh.

"Cheers!" Mike said as he lifted his glass.

"Cheers everyone." Ita toasted.

"Slanta!" Patrick lifted his pint.

"To friendship," said Kathleen.

"To our home." Pauline said quietly.

They brought the full pint glasses to their lips and drank. They all laughed and spoke jovially above the uproar of the room. The evening began.

Kathleen returned with a round of fresh pints for all of them.

The night went on. The band eventually started. Nothing starts on time in Ireland. The room exploded with the sound of pop music and cheering. Keane really loved it. He loved music.

More pints were brought to the table by Ita. The five of them sat in the corner at the small, round table.

When it was all over, the band stopped, the people had gone, and Mike, Kathleen, Ita, Pauline and Patrick, with Mark, were sitting at the table filled with pint glasses.

"Listen, we're going to sneak over to the Aberdeen Arms Hotel for a small party. We have to be careful going in. Patrick, the pubs can only stay open 'till half-eleven. The guardai come and shut everything down if the pubs try to stay open later. It's past that now which is a violation for the Shamrock."

"We'll sneak into the Aberdeen and once we're in we go to the back bar where we won't be seen or heard."

"Grand, Mark." Mike said.

"Oh, lovely. We're all pissed already. But this will be fun." Kathleen said.

"I'm afraid Pauline and I cannot make it. It sounds wonderful but we must go now. Thank you for a great time once again." He stood and reached for Pauline's hand.

They were all sorry that Keane and Pauline could not make it. They understood, though.

They all left the Shamrock, which had been asking them to leave for half an hour now. Mike and Kathleen, and Ita and Mark went up the street to the corner to sneak into the Aberdeen Arms Hotel. Patrick and Pauline went in the other direction.

A few doors down from the Shamrock Inn was Gerry Hartigan's apartment. Keane knocked on the door. A woman answered. Keane explained that they needed Gerry to give them a lift home. The woman was Gerry's daughter, Sandra. She took them back to Kilshanny.

Sunday came and Kenae went to Mass with Maeve.

When Mass was over Keane was walking out of the wooden doors trying to catch up with Maeve who wasted no time in getting to her car.

While trying to catch up with Maeve he heard someone call his name. He stopped in amazement.

"Patrick! Patrick!"

The gentleman was walking quickly toward Keane. He had a woman walking with him.

"Pardon me, you must be Patrick." He said as he caught up with Keane.

"My name is Paul Martin. This is my wife, Kay. We're over on holiday and staying at Maeve's Bed & Breakfast. She had mentioned you to us. We recognized your hat." He said with a slight laugh when mentioning the Akubra.

Keane laughed, too.

"Well, very nice to meet you. I am Patrick Keane, yes. I guess it is the hat." They laughed more.

"So glad we caught up to you, Patrick. How are you getting back?" He asked.

"I was just trying to catch up with Maeve."

"Do ride with us if you'd like. We'd love to drive you back. Perhaps we can get some lunch in that town, Lahinch." Paul said.

"Thank you. I'd love that. I'll just let Maeve know to go without me."

The three of them walked over to Maeve's car.

"Fine, Patrick. I'll see you back at home, then. Bye-bye." She said to all of them.

Back at Tullamore they sat for a moment in the sitting room chatting. Afterward they all went to their rooms to change for the day out.

Keane saw Pauline walk by the dining room. He quickly left his room to speak with her.

"Pauline." He almost yelled her name.

"Patrick. How was Mass?" She asked, glad to see him again.

"It was fine. Maybe one day we'll go together." He said quietly with a shyness in his tone.

"That would be lovely." Pauline said slowly, moved by his tone and his question.

"Perhaps tomorrow we'll have lunch in Ennistymon? If it's fine with you?" He hoped for the right answer.

"Grand.

"That would be lots of fun." She smiled.

"I can't wait." He said honestly.

"That's very nice of you." She said not giving Keane the answer he desired.

"I'll see you in the morning, then, I guess. Bye Pauline." He said slowly.

"Yes. Keep well, Patrick. Have fun today."

"I'm going out to lunch with the people who've recently arrived, Paul and Kay." He explained feeling awkward.

"Oh they're lovely people." Pauline spoke.

"See you tomorrow."

"Bye, Patrick." She said and walked away.

He watched her leave his presence.

"Ready to go Patrick?" Paul's voice boomed out.

"Yes, ready." He was still looking in the direction where Pauline had moved.

Paul, Kay, and Patrick gathered at Paul's car.

Pauline watched as the car rolled down the long farmhouse drive.

9

To Journey in Stages

"Pakie! Pakie!" Maeve bellowed out his name.

Keane was sitting on the downward slope of pasture that overlooked the river. He was playing his whistle while watching the river's water rush by below.

He turned when he heard his name called. The cows moved slowly out of the way as Keane stood and walked up the steep slope. Most of the cows went to the far end of the pasture when Keane came and played his whistle.

Pakie hopped the wood and wire fence and walked up the last stretch of the farmhouse road. He walked under the long branches of the tree in front of Tullamore.

"Pakie!" She bellowed one last time as she saw him coming up the drive.

He was walking up the steps now.

"It's tea, Pakie. Would you like a cup of tea? I know how you like your tea and scones." She said to him as he drew closer.

"Oh, scones you say? That sounds good. Thank you, Maeve. I'll have some tea. I was just sitting below near the river playing my whistle, scaring the cows." He laughed.

"Never mind the lazy beasts. You enjoy yourself. But come in now for some tea. John is inside, too."

Maeve and Pakie went into the house. They passed through the front room and entered the dining room.

"Come, Pakie. The usual place now." Maeve said loudly.

Pakie went through the door into Maeve's private home. He sat in his usual seat at the table.

"Hi John."

John O'Connor was sitting comfortably in his favorite chair near the wood-burning stove.

"Hi Pakie." John answered in his soft, quiet voice.

John could get his voice much louder, though, and do a good bit of yelling. Keane witnessed this one early evening as he was walking down the long farmhouse drive on his way to Ennistymon to the teach ceol. This was the house of music where local musicians and townsfolk come to enjoy themselves with good traditional music and good set dancing.

As Keane walked that early evening he spotted a small herd of cows standing lazily on the farmhouse drive. They had broken through the fence again. Keane stopped and the cows stared at him. He picked up a nearby stick and walked close to them and gave a short yell and a pound of the stick to the ground. The cows groaned loudly and moved slowly. Keane stepped quickly and went behind them with whoops and yells hitting the stick on the ground. The cows now moved with frantic speed back into the fenced-in area. But a few of the cows, the leaders Keane thought, were running up the hill. Keane followed but they were now cornered in the small house below that belonged to Tullamore. They could cause some damage, Keane thought, if he tried to get them now. He went back to Tullamore and told John and Mark what had happened.

"Oh, they're at it again, eh? Thanks Pakie."

John and Mark went quickly out the door. Pakie followed them.

At the small house below John took his stick and yelled loudly at the cows.

"You bitch. Get back. Get back, bitch!" And the cows slunk their heads down and walked with John and Mark to the broken fence. Keane never before saw John yell. But, Keane thought it must be frustrating dealing with the cows on a daily basis.

Maeve brought Pakie his cup of tea. She brought a small plate full of scones on her return trip to the table.

"Now." Maeve placed the dish down.

"Oh, look at those scones. Thank you, Maeve." He grabbed a scone and it disappeared into his mouth.

"I heard you playin' dat whistle, Pakie. You make a pleasant sound wit it." John said.

"Thanks, John. I love music. I may not play very well but I keep trying. I think I'm going to get a bodhran while I'm here. I have one at home that I didn't bring. Maybe I'll go to Ennis."

"Maybe Pauline would like to go with you, Pakie."
Maeve smiled at him.

"Yes, you're right. Maybe she would enjoy the trip."
Keane acted as if he didn't understand.

"She's a fine girl, Pakie." Maeve persisted.

Keane sipped his tea and ate a scone.

"Yes, she is a wonderful person."

"You haven't seen the Donohue girls in some time, Pakie." Maeve mentioned.

She calls them the Donohue girls even though Kathleen has been married for two years now.

"Yes, they've disappeared. I'm sure I'll see them again, though."

"I think Paul and Kay are much better for ye. There's nothing wrong with the Donohue girls now, Pakie, don't get me wrong, but Paul and Kay won't be keepin' ye out 'till six in the mornin'."

Keane laughed at that.

"The four of you get along very well, I think." She persisted.

"Oh they are both very good people. I enjoy their company immensely. It was good of them to ask me along to Galway with them. What a great trip."

"I think you had better eat in here again tomorrow, Pakie. We're very full. And those people are coming back for a night, maybe two, God help us."

Pakie had been eating in Maeve's kitchen for a time now. She invited him in one morning because she and John got to know him so well in his stay at Tullamore. He was alone and that had Maeve watch out for him, too. As for Keane, he was overjoyed about eating in a home, rather than alone, or perhaps, with strangers.

The real joy stemmed from the fact that Pauline would be nearer to him as he ate his breakfast. He was able to watch her motion, to see her as she moved about the kitchen getting this or setting down that. With each movement she passed Keane with a smile or a touch of her soft, small hand on his shoulder.

Maeve saw it all. She never missed a look or a smile or the quickest touch. She managed to keep a busy face on, pretending not to notice. She was very busy, too, cooking and getting breakfast prepared for all the different types of guests now crowding her dining room. But she never missed a communication, silent or otherwise, between the two. When she knew it was safe she smiled about the goings on between Pauline and Keane. It was part pretext that

Maeve had Keane eat in the private kitchen. She knew a match when she saw one.

'Pakie.' Keane took the new name willingly and happily.

"Pakie. I think I'll call you that from now on. It's an old Irish name for Patrick. Pakie." Maeve had told him one day.

"Oh, I love the name. Pakie. Yeah, I've heard the name." Keane smiled, feeling that much closer to home.

The name stuck. And Patrick became Pakie. Pauline smiled at the new name, and decided she, too, would call him Pakie.

As they both walked through Lahinch others that Keane had come to know in his travels through Galvin's Pub and Kenny's Pub and other places now called him 'Pakie.' Now when Keane went down the street of Lahinch he would hear "Hi Pakie, how are you?" He would answer as if born with the name.

It was another beautiful morning, sun-filled, soft hue of green shining through the windows of Tullamore as Keane sat in the kitchen eating his breakfast.

"I haven't any work today at Foley's." She looked at him hopefully.

"Fantastic!" He exclaimed wide-eyed.

"Would you like to go to Lahinch? It's a lovely morning and perhaps it will stay this way." He asked her.

"I want to take you somewhere. If you don't mind, Pakie." She said to him seriously.

"I'll go." Keane answered. "Should I know?" He asked.

"Of course. I want to take you to the Cliffs. It's so beautiful overlooking the ocean." Pauline explained.

"Oh, I would love that very much. I haven't been there yet."

They were both speaking of the Cliffs of Moher. It is the edge of Europe itself.

"I was hopin, now, Pakie, that you haven't gone there in all of your walkin'." She smiled.

"Not yet. And I'm glad of it. Now I can see the Cliffs with you." He said looking into her eyes that were drawing him deeper into herself.

Pauline touched his shoulder with her hand and ran her gentle fingers smoothly over to the other shoulder. She bent down to him and placed her soft lips on his cheek and kissed him.

"Pauline."

Pakie said her name softly. She had never kissed him.

Then she quickly darted across the kitchen to gather plates. She didn't look at him as she went out of the room into the busy dining area.

Maeve had been looking in from the back window as she gathered some plants. She saw everything. She smiled and was very happy for Keane. He seems so alone, she thought. And, of course, she knew Pauline was alone. Dear girl, she thought again.

Pauline came back into the kitchen carrying more plates, empty this time. She still didn't look at Keane.

"Paul and Kay are asking about you." She said to him.

"I'm going to say good morning to them. I'll be right back." He got up and went through the doors.

The dining room was crowded. Every table was taken by guests. Paul and Kay sat near the large window that looked out into the front room. They sat where Keane used to sit. He walked over to them.

"Good morning, Paul. Hi Kay."

"Good morning, Patrick." Paul said in his strong voice.

"Another brilliant day, isn't it, Patrick?" Paul announced.

"We've been fortunate to miss the rain." Paul continued.

"Since I've been here it's only been some mornings and evenings of mist. Nothing more." Keane replied.

"What are your plans, Patrick?" He asked.

"After Pauline finishes here we're going to the Cliffs."

"Oh that is a lovely spot to visit. So dramatic." Kay spoke.

"Yes, it is, indeed. Mind your step on those trails now." Paul added.

"How about we meet for dinner tonight? In Lahinch? Hill that suit your plans?" Keane hoped.

"That sounds terrific. Will Pauline be joining us?" Paul asked.

"Yes. She would enjoy coming with us. Pauline loves your company very much."

"Well, then. It sounds like you have a lovely day ahead with a lovely young lady. And we'll meet tonight at seven in Lahinch. How about the Shamrock?" Paul asked.

"Great. Seven sounds fine. If I don't see you back here before Lahinch, I'll see you in town. Have a good day." He said.

Keane turned and went back into the kitchen.

"He looks so happy, doesn't he, dear?" Kay stated.

When Keane sat back down there was a fresh cup of coffee waiting.

"I'll get your food now. I've kept it warm for you." Pauline said.

"After the Cliffs would you like to have dinner with Paul and Kay?"

"I would love that, Pakie. Thank you. What time?"

"At seven in Lahinch at the Shamrock. Is that a good time?"

"Lovely. I enjoy the Shamrock." She smiled and walked briskly to the dining room carrying plates and a light heart.

"Patrick! Why aren't you driving a car? All Americans love their cars!" Gerry Hartigan laughed as he drove Pauline and Keane to the Cliffs.

"I mean, all the tourists come here driving all over Ireland, most of them badly at that." He laughed again.

"I decided before I arrived here that I would see how it goes for a while without a car. I've enjoyed it. I do have to get one, however, as I have things I must do before I leave." He explained.

Pauline looked across at him. Her long hair falling loosely over her shoulders. It was not tied back as it was most other times.

"Don't get me wrong, Patrick." Gerry said.

"This is my livelihood and I enjoy it. I'll drive you or anyone anywhere." He continued.

Gerry Hartigan, married man, father, taxi driver, has been to every spot at the Cliffs. He has climbed every trail. He is just as familiar with all of the Burren. He knows every inch of the rock that covers a large territory of County Clare. Gerry Hartigan, fifty- two years old, has climbed Crough Patrick several times. He could speak of this land with the best of them.

"Where ya goin' Pauline?" Gerry asked her.

"I'm going to the South Trail. It's a lovely day. Not as much wind." She answered.

"That's your spot, Pauline. That's yours alright. It's been yours for a long time. I don't even go there any more fearin' I'd have to pay ye rent for it now." He joked.

Pauline laughed, too. She has seen him at the Cliffs many times. He walked sometimes with his wife or with his daughter, Sandra. Pauline just assumed that Gerry Hartigan must have seen her as well.

The white passenger van that Gerry drove pulled up in one of the large lots near the cliffs. It was a crowded day, like most days that didn't rain.

"Got lots of tourists out here today, Patrick." Gerry said.

"We'll be goin' where they won't. They just want their snapshots and then they leave on their buses for God knows where." Pauline said.

She was right about the tourists. Very few of them ventured far from the souvenir shop.

Pauline and Keane climbed out of the van.

"I'll be back in about two hours for the both of you now. If you need, ring me sooner. Keep well. Mind yourselves now."

Gerry waved and turned the van around heading back toward Lahinch.

"We'll go this way now, Pakie."

She took his hand and led him onto the footpath. The wind was blowing steadily but not as full as it could be blowing.

Pauline, holding Pakie's hand, led them both off of the footpath onto the muddy path. They walked passed the few tourists that dared to venture out beyond souvenir grabbing. Not long off they were on their own.

Pauline's hair was blowing freely in the steady wind. Keane took off his hat.

Keane looked at her as she led him down the earthy path. She looked more beautiful than he had ever seen her. She was not at all like the Pauline who worked at the B & B. She was different. She was somehow different.

"Isn't it lovely? Isn't it wild, Pakie?"

She turned to him letting go of his hand and pointing at the sea crashing into the dark, craggy shelf of rock that was the edge of Ireland.

The cliffs climbed out of the ocean like a wild beast. The sea relentlessly pounded into the high cliffs. They rose some eight hundred feet above the turbulent sea.

"This is so dramatic. So spectacular to watch." Keane said as he stood in the steady wind with a slight mist falling on both of them.

The wind carried the mist of the crashing waves up above the cliffs to spill over onto the pastures.

"Come, follow me." Pauline grabbed his hand once more, held it tightly, and continued in their sally for her place.

It was a place in which she came to so many times. Often she would draw the cliffs as she huddled in her walled place high above the rushing, roaring waves. The crashing ocean was the sound of fury. A rage against that which would not budge. Only the pounding of centuries could change what would otherwise never change. Nature in its rawest state needs to change. The sea was doing the best that nature could provide as agent of change.

The muddy, slippery path narrowed as they went on. At the Cliffs of Moher there were no fences anywhere. When someone walked to the edge or very near the edge on one of the many paths there was nothing to stop them from falling or from protecting them from the strong pulling and pushing winds that tore off of the open ocean.

Where Pauline took Keane was the most dangerous of the paths. There were twists and turns where one wrong step could lead straight into danger and this danger was not retractable. The many people who developed these paths from the natural landscape were as relentless as the raging sea attempting to conquer that which would not move or change. The pursuit for beauty is a formidable task arduous in its nature, heroic in its rewards. Pauline in her gentle covering of a frail, delicate, and tender nature sought out the rugged, untamed beauty in her place at the cliffs.

She saw the same characteristics in Keane. Pauline saw in his soul the quiet strength of resolve. She watched him many times when she passed by and he was sitting on that stone wall that was his place. He would stare out at the land he loved but she knew he was looking inward. Looking at his soul, feeling lost and feeling found at the same time. She saw him in church, too. The strength it took to understand the needs of others. She was drawn to him by these rare characteristics. She only waited patiently for Keane to tell her what he saw inside of himself. For what was he searching?

She didn't mind his hat, either. It made her giggle.

"Mind your step now, Pakie."

"We've arrived. Just step through here." She took his hand as she stood still.

Keane stepped through a shelter of rock walls. It was a small space that looked out onto the green-blue of the ocean pushing itself hard against the rugged, unmoving earth.

"Isn't it beautiful? This is my secret place, Patrick."

She looked at him. She took both of his hands into her soft, gentle palms. She closed her tiny fingers around them.

"Do you like it here? Tell me you do. I know you do. Isn't it lovely and wild at the same time?" She spoke quietly as she looked into his hazel eyes.

"Very lovely and very beautiful." Keane spoke slowly, entranced by the moment and by Pauline.

Keane stepped in as close to Pauline as he has ever been. With his hands in hers he drew them closer together pulling their hands up between them. Her face was close to his. One slight pull on her hands brought her to him forever. He kissed her soft lips as the roaring waves crashed against the iron-still earth.

The strong ocean breeze pulled and tugged at Paul and Kay as they walked the beach path at Lahinch. It was almost seven and they were heading toward the Shamrock. They had discovered this sandy path that Keane had walked on when he first arrived. Paul and Kay walked on it daily at this hour. This was their place as Keane had his on the stone wall in the valley as Pauline had hers in the cliffs. Everyone belonged somewhere. Everyone had their place.

The story of Abraham places attention on the sense of belonging as its axis of meaning. It was the heart of the story which illustrated belonging. The spiritual journey of Abraham manifested in land, the physical sense of belonging. Abraham was the great patriarch to a people without land, without belonging. They looked to Abraham for hope.

Paul hugged his wife on the sandy path above the large, craggy rocks that kept back the ocean. The wind blew between them but they held on tight. They have been married for twenty-five years. He met his wife when he was thirty years of age. She had moved to England for work. He lived in the peaceful village of Lichfield in Staffordshire County. A lovely town with a history dating back beyond the tenth century. They had no children but they had each other.

Pauline and Keane entered the Shamrock Inn just before seven. They went into the formal dining room.

Pauline spotted Paul and Kay sitting at a rear table. The place was not crowded.

"Pauline! Good to see you!" Paul spoke in his strong tones of cheerfulness. He stood to greet her.

"Hi Patrick. Happy to see you." He continued.

"Good evening." Pauline said to both of them.

"Hi Paul. Hi Kay." Keane said.

Keane pulled out the chair for Pauline. The four of them sat as the candle in the middle of the table illuminated their happiness.

"Pauline, how were the cliffs today?" Paul asked.

Kay looked at the two of them knowing that something had changed, something had occurred.

"They were grand. The weather was cooperating for a change. It was windy but not so bad as other days."

"There are so many trails. Kay and I did not want to venture that far off when we were there." He looked at them with a smile.

"I have this place that I go to which is fairly distant from the tourist area. It's quite dangerous to walk on. Some days I've turned back due to the strong winds. On those narrow trails the wind and the wet ground are too dangerous a combination. But today we managed. I think it was the best day for the cliffs." She said and smiled slightly as she glanced at Keane.

Kay smiled, too. She knew and understood.

"There's some fantastic music in town, Patrick." Paul changed the subject before everyone turned to smiling.

"I've discovered a great place to go and have a very good time with local musicians. It's in Ennistymon." Keane told them.

"Eugene's Pub is it, Patrick?" Paul asked.

"That's a good place, too. But this isn't a pub. It's an old Protestant church used as a town center. It's at the bottom of the street. It's the Teach Ceol. The House of Music. They have about six or seven musicians led by Joe Rinn on fiddle. His two children bring their instruments. His son is on concertina, very good, too. The daughter is on fiddle. There are others. Whoever wants to join in is welcome."

"That sounds brilliant. I haven't heard of it. When is it?" Paul asked excitedly.

"There's one tonight. We were hoping you'd want to go. They serve scones and tea and there's set dancing and waltzing. It's really community oriented. Sometimes there are people visiting who join in with a song if they have one. It's been my favorite place. I enjoy the pubs but it gets tiring to go with all the crowds."

"How about that, Kay?" Paul asked his wife.

"It sounds lovely. I'd love for all of us to go." She answered.

The four of them conversed on different subjects as they ate their dinner. The candle flickered its small light enough to portray the friendship glowing on the four faces.

"Which university did you attend to attain your Doctor's degree, Patrick?" Paul asked.

"I went to a small state school for my undergraduate work. History major. Then I went off to seminary, Union Theological Seminary in Manhattan. From there I went to Yale University, school of religion. Many of the classes were held at Yale Divinity School. I was very surprised to get my acceptance letter. I studied Old Testament, referred to today as Hebrew bible. It was fascinating. I wrote my dissertation on the Abraham cycle of stories. Focusing on belonging, land, and the deep-set spiritual journey we are all on, known and unknown, manifesting in land and belonging. Have I put anyone to sleep yet?" He laughed.

"That's brilliant, Patrick. Brilliant! At Union Seminary did you become a minister?" Paul asked.

"No. I did get my Master's of Divinity degree. But eventually I went back to my Catholic roots. It started for me at Union so I decided not to seek ordination but an academic standing.

"And I had been at Hope for about eleven years now. Loretta and myself." Keane laughed.

"Loretta had been working in the seminary bookstore for some twenty years. It seemed she and I were all alone at the seminary. She has retired now, thankfully."

"What will you do next?" Paul asked.

Pauline looked at Keane with the slightest movement of her eyes, narrowing almost unnoticeably.

Kay looked at Pauline.

"I'm thinking of plans now. I have to finalize things soon. I think before I leave I'll know."

"When are you going, Patrick?" Paul asked.

"I'll be leaving in a few weeks. I'm on the other side of my holiday now. The first half I spent walking the land. I was climbing the hills of Kilshanny. It was a type of revitalization for me, a rallying of soul. Now, this stage of my journey has to do with belonging. I found friends, one very, very special to me," Keane looked at Pauline, she looked at him and answered with a smile.

"The both of you have been very kind to me. And I consider you my friends. My holiday has been in stages. It's truly been wonderful." Keane looked at all of them.

"Cheers, Patrick." Paul lifted his glass. Everyone followed and sipped their drinks.

"Paul and I appreciate that, Patrick. And you are our friend. Both you and Pauline, who is so lovely." Kay spoke with her Dublin accent.

"Thank you." Keane replied.

When dinner was over the four of them got into Paul's car. They drove the short distance from Lahinch to Ennistymon.

"Oh, yes. We've driven passed this church a few times now, haven't we dear?" Paul said.

He drove his car through the open, high, wrought- iron fence surrounding the tall brick and stone structure of the former Protestant church.

"Yes. I've wondered about it. I've even seen the sign but haven't remembered my Irish." Kay admitted.

At the door of the Teach Ceol Keane was greeted by Larkin O'Connor. Larkin owned the general store in Ennistymon, O'Connor's, which hosted the Post Office in the rear of the store. Larkin and his wife, Ena, operated the store with both of them switching roles as Postal clerks.

"Hello, Patrick." Larkin said.

Larkin was a big man who spoke under his breath in a mumbled speech.

"Hello, Larkin. Good to see you again." Patrick said.

"Good evening, Miss O'Sullivan." Said Larkin.

"These are my friends, Paul and Kay Martin." Keane said.

"Hello and welcome to Teach Ceol. I'm sure you'll have a splendid time." Larkin said.

"Four of us, Larkin, please." Keane said as he readied to pay the admission.

"Grand. That's eight pounds, then." Larkin said.

"Patrick, no, please." Paul said.

Keane gave the coins to Larkin and they all went inside the large, open room.

"Please, you've already paid for dinner, Paul. This is small in comparison." Keane said as they entered the room.

There were people already gathered inside. Some were seated on chairs in scattered rows. Others were sitting on the bleacher-type seats on the one side of the spacious room.

The four of them got situated with their seating and then walked around the room to greet people.

Joe Rinn came over to Keane.

"Good evening, Patrick Keane. It's wonderful that you've made it again. You're quite a regular to our irregular nights. And Miss O'Sullivan is with you. Lovely." Joe spoke in a deep and quiet voice.

"And these are my two friends, Paul and Kay Martin. They're also staying at Tullamore."

"Lovely. It's a beautiful part of the county. I'm glad everyone came tonight."

"Good evening, Miss O'Sullivan." Joe said as Pauline came near from speaking with others.

"Mr. Rinn. Lovely night." Pauline said quietly.

"I must take my leave now to get the band in a lively mood. Enjoy yourselves." Joe said and went toward the gathered musicians already sounding their instruments.

"My first night here," Keane began to explain.

"I was standing in front at the gate waiting for Paddy to pick me up. Well, he never came and everyone was leaving. The rain started lightly and it was quite a walk back to Tullamore. But fortunately I didn't have to walk. Joe Rinn and his family pulled up at the gate and asked if I was alright. I explained about Paddy and Joe kindly offered to take me back to Tullamore. A very kind and gentle man. And a hell of a fiddle player. He plays with the Four Courts which is a famous traditional band in Ireland."

"He's a lovely man. I've known him and his family for some time now." Pauline said.

"That's what the Teach Ceol is all about. Community. Keeping alive a culture and knowing your neighbor." Keane said.

The music started with the bright timbre of Joe Rinn's fiddle playing. The room shifted abruptly in mood from one of quiet conversations to a lively, spirited climate. The room became playful as the band played its reels and jigs.

When the band came around to playing waltzes the clatter of chairs being moved filled the air. Everyone waltzed. Pauline and Pakie held each other as they moved in three-quarter time over the floor. Pauline was a very good dancer. Keane was a bit rusty. But it didn't matter at the Teach Ceol.

When the music broke for a pause the ladies with the help of the men brought out long folding tables to set up for tea and scones. Everyone gathered around the table for some hot tea and different flavored, fresh baked scones.

When everyone had gotten their tea and scones and resettled into their seats Joe raised his voice above the hum of conversation.

"Patrick. Patrick Keane. Would you do us another song as you did the other evening? We've still got the guitar." Joe smiled.

He knew he was putting Keane on the spot. But Keane responded as Joe knew he would.

"I'd love to play a tune, Joe Rinn. Thank you."

He took a good gulp of hot tea and walked over to the guitar.

He picked it up and sat on the stool near the band.

He strummed it a few times to get comfortable.

Pauline watched Keane with delight as he readied his song. Her face was a radiant glow as her long dark hair surrounded her fair featured face.

"This is a song from the North which I love to hear and sing." Keane said to introduce Ragland Road, a longtime favorite of Ireland.

Keane disappeared into the song. The quiet man gave way to the lyrics and the tune. What emerged was the soul of the man.

"He's very good, actually, Pauline." Paul said quietly to Pauline sitting next to him.

"Oh, lovely. He sings this one lovely." Kay said.

When it was over everyone sipping their tea and eating scones were clapping appreciatively of Keane's choice of song. The Irish love their music. And no one has to be an expert or a professional at bringing a song to life.

Keane still sat there holding the guitar picking notes out thinking of another tune to give them.

He chose another well-known and highly loved song by Ireland's favorite, Christy Moore. Keane strummed and picked the first few chords and everyone clapped.

Pauline smiled broadly. Keane looked at her and sang Nancy Spain. No one moved, not a sip, nor a bite.

It wasn't Keane himself that brought the crowd to halting silence. It was the song. It was so popular in Ireland.

Keane glanced sideways at Joe Rinn and caught his eye. Keane nodded his head slightly. Joe placed the fiddle in position and when it was time the melody overflowed from his bow. When he was near finished with the solo bit his son Aiden repeated the melody on his concertina. The three of them finished out the song to loud applause.

"One more," Larkin yelled out. Keane smiled.

"Thank you very much every one. I don't want to overstay my welcome." Keane laughed at his little joke.

"Here's one from the American repertoire."

He played one of his favorite Bob Dylan tunes, Shelter from the Storm.

Keane finished the song and thanked everyone for letting him sing a few songs. He placed the guitar back in its case and walked passed Joe.

"Thanks, Joe. I loved doing them."

The night continued on with more vibrant jigs and reels from Joe Rinn and company with Pakie sitting in on a few tunes playing the bodhran owned by Mary, a young lady he met there the first night.

Soon everyone was set dancing which even Keane attempted to do for a tune.

Pauline made the rounds in the sets dancing with Larkin, Paul and others. It was fun and the craic was good, Keane thought.

The rare Irish sun belied its reputation as an absence in the often rainy skies. Keane stepped out in its earliest light. He walked down the long, winding farmhouse drive as was by now his custom. His steps were the only sound with the exception of the sheep running through the field in which they were grazing.

Keane walked on the narrow, bony road that rose and fell delivering velvet landscapes of green hues wet with the morning dew. The white, narrow spire of the Kilshanny church rose starkly out of the sunlit greens of the pastures. He arrived at the wrought-iron gate and peered at the church.

It offered him peace and with devotion Keane's understanding seeped deeper. When Keane locked himself into one perspective of the church all the other dimensions of the church became lost to him. Through devotion, not only academic understanding, the full measure of the body of the church became known. An erudite understanding was limiting to the truth of the church and bullied faith aside with reason. As Keane peered at the metamorphic church he saw a distinct difference than had been his thinking not long ago. The distinction was devotion.

Keane entered its sanctuary and stepped into the back pew. He entered into prayer as he knelt in the pew.

The prayer was for understanding.

On his walk back to Tullamore he paused at the narrow, dirt road which took him to his place in the valley. He looked up its long, steep hill almost studying its height. He turned to the ascent and went to its height and down again with the sun on his back and the pastures lit to bright hues of green. He walked passed his place on the stone wall where music met pasture and peace laid rest his soul.

He stopped at Pauline's house and turned onto the walk that led him to her front door. He knocked on her door.

Pauline was brushing her hair and thought she heard the door, but it couldn't be, she thought. But the knock came again. It wasn't a soft knock, gentle or angelic. It was the knock of decision, not loud but firm.

She placed her brush down on her bureau and went to the door, looking with a quick glance at herself in the mirror that hung in her hallway.

"Pakie!" Pauline looked at Patrick standing there at her door. She smiled and touched his hand.

"I'm so happy you've come." She waved her other hand slowly indicating the welcome to enter.

"Please do come in, Pakie."

"Good morning, Pauline. I'm sure I'm bothering you at this hour."

"Not at' tall, not at' tall. Never a bother now.

"Did you walk to the church this morning?" She asked.

"Yes. And on my way back I stopped at the road that cuts passed Tullamore and brings me to the stone wall. I knew I had to come here then. I had to come and see you. Now, this morning, at this hour." He tried to explain himself.

He stepped forward and placed his hands in hers and brought her to him with a gentle lead of her hands. In a motion he was holding her tightly in his arms.

Everything he ever dreamed, or felt, thought, or yearned for, was now pressed against him in his arms. All the things some one can be for Patrick was Pauline.

"I don't feel so all alone any longer, Patrick."

She whispered it so softly in his ear as they held each other.

"Nor do I, Pauline." He said the words out loud.

The words that were waiting to be spoken all these many, lonely years were now said.

Patrick lifted his hands placing them on either side of her face while looking deeply into her eyes. He brought her closer and kissed her. It was a long, life- fulfilling kiss. Their lips together found hope as they found each other.

Pauline's eyes swelled with the tears that other times often fell with the longing of a loneliness that could not be answered. Now the wetness forming in her eyes came from the radiant joy of a journey now over and a journey triumphant.

10

You Shall Be Blessed

"You were brilliant last night, Pakie." Pauline said.

They had left Pauline's house and walked down the long stretch of the narrow, bony road that Keane walked so many times. They were walking toward Tullamore where the giant Terebinth tree stands protectively over the lives who know its shelter.

"Hey, let's stand on the rock, Pauline."

He led her as they climbed atop the great stone wall. Patrick put his arm around the waist of Pauline drawing her close as they looked out on the great valley enhanced by the rise and fall of the distant hills.

Patrick tightened his embrace with Pauline and turned himself to face her. It was as natural as the breath that filled the narrow space between them. It was as if they never knew anything else at this moment but for the two of them.

Their faces fell together as if all the years of loneliness pressed them together as a natural and evolutionary moment. The kiss filled each one of them; one to another, another to one. And as all love makes it, time for that moment stood still.

"Pakie, play me an air. One that you love." Pauline said with a smile. Her arms were wrapped around Keane's waist.

Keane took out his whistle and blew a few notes. He played an air, slow and melodic, eyes closed as the rare Irish sun illuminated the lush valley.

The morning breeze blew between them and through Pauline's long, dark hair which hung down freely.

"Lovely, Patrick." Pauline spoke quietly.

Keane put the whistle back on his lips and played a fast and rollicking jig. Pauline laughed aloud tilting her head back as her long, dark hair swung behind her.

She started to dance on the long, flat, stone wall. She danced a fair jig as Keane watched and played. All the happiness that Pauline had kept inside of her came out in this moment. That is, all the happiness kept silent and waiting for the proper moment to have it shown.

The jig finished and Pauline leaped toward Keane falling into his arms. They both laughed aloud as the morning surrounded them in sun and breeze.

They held hands as they walked up the steep hill on the narrow, dirt road. They walked passed the barn which stood at the top of the hill. The dogs were still outside sniffing around in the same places. The sound of metal and voices came from within the barn.

At the bottom of the narrow, dirt road Keane stopped. Tullamore stood high and lofty behind them.

"I wonder if we have time to walk to the church now?" He asked Pauline.

"Oh, we'll make time. That's a lovely idea, Pakie." And they walked in the other direction instead of going toward Tullamore.

They both stood at the wrought-iron gate of the Kilshanny church.

"Pauline, I love it here at the doors of the church."

He looked at the white building with the narrow spire climbing high with the cross reaching further.

"Pakie, it's not a bad thing to love. But do come inside instead of standing at the door."

She pulled open the black, wrought-iron gate. She led him inside.

Keane stopped at the back pew where he normally sat. But Pauline tugged on his hand.

"Follow me, Pakie." She whispered. And she led him to the front pew.

Pauline fell freely to one knee at the head of the pew. She paused and thoughtfully gave the sign of the cross. Each point of contact she made with her hand to her head, heart and the connection of the two across the body, filled and sustained her very soul.

Keane watched with deep wonder at the natural devotion Pauline held.

Keane fell to one knee, paused, slowly did the sign of the cross and gave a silent prayer for understanding. The two of them knelt together in the pew, side by side, hand in hand, and prayed for a short while.

Pauline raised Patrick up and brought him near the alter.

"We'll light two candles. One for us, in hope, one for Paul and Kay, in friendship." And she lit one candle and handed the flame to Patrick who lit the next candle. She knelt tugging Patrick with her and they prayed.

Rising they saw Father Kelly coming.

"Good morning, Father." Pauline said.

"Good morning, Father Kelly." Keane also said.

"Devotion is wonderful, isn't it, Patrick?" Father Kelly said peacefully.

"In your profession, Patrick, it's so much of the book work, so much of the academic. It's wonderful to come to devotion where the books converge with faith."

"You're a good girl, Pauline." He placed his hand on her arm, shook it lightly and moved it to Keane's shoulder.

"God bless and good morning." He walked through the door and went to the yard in the rear of the church.

"Maybe I'll get a car today, Pauline." Keane said on the narrow, bony road back.

"If you like. I'm happy to walk with you. I love the hills, too."

Pauline didn't think much about a car or driving.

"If you're not too busy today at Foley's perhaps we'll get Gerry Hartigan to take us to Shannon. I can rent one at the airport." Keane explained.

"That would be grand. I'd love to go for the ride."

"Then we'll take a ride down the coast. I haven't been there yet. What do you say?" He asked her.

"It'd be fun to get away and see the coast. Down the way to Kilkee is absolutely lovely. It's clouding up a bit, Pakie. The sun seems to be acting more itself under Irish skies." She looked up.

"But Kilkee is lovely in rain or shine." Pauline added.

Pauline and Keane walked up the long, winding farmhouse road holding hands. Pauline was pointing out different things in the landscape and pointing toward Lahinch. They stood under the Terebinth tree as Pauline and Keane watched a newborn calf suckling her mother.

Maeve stopped by the window in the front sitting room as she walked by to get to the kitchen. She saw Pauline and Patrick standing under the large tree. They were still holding hands and laughing. Maeve's smile grew on her face to its broadest reaches. She loved Pauline and cared dearly for her. And Keane she admired and this appreciation was growing.

The two souls walked into Tullamore. Maeve was waiting for them.

"And what are you two early birds doing?"

Pauline took a step toward Maeve and quickly put her arms around her neck and kissed her on the cheek.

"Good morning, Maeve. Lovely mornin' now, isn't 'it?" And Pauline disappeared quickly into the dining room and through the door to the kitchen.

Maeve stood surprised and a bit embarrassed.

"Well, Pakie, I think you'd better have your breakfast in the kitchen. Come." Maeve sounded out the order.

"Good morning Paul, Kay." Keane said as he went to their table in the crowded dining room.

"Patrick. Brilliant night. I thoroughly enjoyed myself last evening." Paul said enthusiastically.

"You're so talented, Patrick." Kay complemented him.

"Thank you. I love the Teach Ceol. I'm so glad you had a good time. The people are wonderful and they know how to have fun." Keane said.

"Please sit, Patrick. Join us. Have you had your breakfast yet? I guess you have. There's no getting you out of the kitchen now, is there, Patrick?" Paul laughed.

Keane smiled while pulling the chair closer to the table.

"She's such a lovely woman, Patrick. She is really." Kay couldn't help but mention it.

"What are you up to today?" Paul asked.

"I'm not sure. If Pauline hasn't much to do at Foley's market in town we intend to go to Shannon and get a car. We were thinking of going down the coast to Kilkee. I hear it's a beautiful drive. I think it would be great if you change your plans to join us."

"Patrick, we can take you to get the car this morning if you like. Shannon isn't that far. If by then Pauline is free from her obligations we can all go to Kilkee. We've been meaning to head that way anyway. Here's our chance." Paul said with delight.

"That would be great. Alright, we'll go down to Shannon this morning and take care of business at that point. It shouldn't involve much time. Thank you." Keane said as he reached for a scone in a basket on the table.

"Wonderful! So, we're settled."

"Did you take your walk to the church this morning?" Kay asked.

"Yes, I did. And Pauline came with me. I love that walk so very much. I see all of Ireland on that road to the church and back. I don't feel the need to see the entire country on a bus or even in a car. The whole of Ireland lies from this spot, Tullamore, to the church. I have met so many people in a short time within a short distance. The farmers, I see them on their tractors, I see them on their land. The children are all playing in the fields at different times. I have seen this community at worship during Mass on Sundays and sometimes I've been there on Friday and Saturday nights, too. All the animals are out in the pastures. When I've been out walking I have had people stop and ask if I need a ride. I've been stopped for over thirty minutes at times just to talk about the weather or something simple. I have seen all of Ireland on my walk to the church and back." Keane spoke and then stopped to look at them both.

"I'm sorry. I've gone on too much. I should eat more scones." He laughed.

"Not at all, Patrick. We're glad your holiday has been so very good for you." Paul said.

Paul and Kay finished their breakfast in the lively dining room. Keane stepped back into the kitchen and sat down.

"More coffee, Pakie?" Maeve asked.

"I'll have another cup, thank you, Maeve. Where's John?"

"He's laying down, Pakie. He doesn't feel well. His leg is actin' up." She said trying to conceal a concerned voice.

"I see. Will he need a doctor?"

"I may take him into town, Pakie. We'll see."

"Maeve, will you need my help? I'm here to help you."

"Now, now, Pakie. You're on holiday. Just enjoy yourself."

"Now Maeve, you know I am not the tourist type. I'm here to help if you need me. Please.

"I'm going this morning to Shannon to get a car. Later, after Pauline gets off from Foley's we may go down the coast to Kilkee." Keane explained.

"Paul and Kay taking you to Shannon, Pakie?"

"Yes. And they will join Pauline and me to Kilkee if we go. But I want to make sure you can manage with taking John to the doctor."

"Pakie, Mark is here if need be. You go. When you get home I'll tell you what happened if anything. Now, enough of this. Have your coffee." She poured Keane a full cup of coffee.

Pauline came back into the kitchen from the hectic dining room. She bent down at the waist behind Patrick and surprised him with a quick kiss on the cheek.

"What is this going on in my kitchen now? You two love birds behave yourselves!"

Maeve laughed and received pleasure from seeing the two of them get on so well.

Maeve gathered plates filled with breakfast food from the counter.

"Pauline, I'll bring these out for the larger group."

"Grand. Thank you, Maeve."

"I just spoke with Paul and Kay. They offered to take me to Shannon for the car. And if you are free this afternoon the four of us can travel down the coast to Kilkee. Would that be alright with you?" He asked her as she moved around the kitchen gathering what she needed for the guests.

She stepped quickly over to Keane and kissed him on the cheek.

"I've never been happier. It would be lovely for the four of us to take a trip. I'm sure John-Joe hasn't much work for me today. The hotels are not as busy at the moment."

John-Joe was John Joseph Foley the kind proprietor of Foley's market. He and his wife, Bridy, worked hard and were very kind to Pauline.

Back in his room Keane straightened out his things that had been gathering from neglect.

He lifted the photograph off of the window ledge and looked at it.

The young woman and the young man holding each other glancing at a moment of which only they knew the meaning. Their faces portraying sadness juxtaposed against the festive occasion which led them to dance.

Keane thought about the reason he came to Ireland. It was more than just a holiday. He thought about home. Soon he would be going to that place so distant and so near. Would Pauline go with him? Should he bring Pauline? Keane thought of many questions in that moment.

He placed the old photograph in its beautiful wood frame on the window sill. The young couple, looking away from each other, remained still.

Keane still wondered what that moment meant for each of them. He felt a very strong need to know. He peered at the photograph as he had done so many times before looking for the answer.

The moment was at hand when Keane must face homeward and leave behind his past where he built a protective place to hide. This place held no sense of belonging for him.

After some time Paul and Kay found Keane sitting in his favorite chair in the front sitting room. It was a very handsome room and Keane felt very comfortable sitting in it.

"Patrick! It looks as if you're ready." Paul spoke in his strong voice.

Keane stood and greeted them again.

"Yes. I was just sitting comfortably in my chair."

"We're ready, then, Patrick. It looks as if the weather is changing." Paul said looking out the high windows of the front room.

They drove down the long, winding farmhouse road on their way to Shannon. It was now raining but Ireland looked wonderful in a new way in the rain.

Paul, Kay, and Patrick sat with intervals of silence and conversation. It was a comfortable silence accompanied by the views of the countryside.

"We'll be leaving in a few days, Patrick." Paul finally said.

The statement was filled with information for Keane. They had all become friends from the very first meeting. Keane knew they had to get back, of course, but he couldn't picture that event nor had he envisioned it. Something drained from him as he sat in the backseat of the car.

"When do you go back?" This was all Keane could manage to speak.

"On Monday morning, Patrick. It's hard to believe for Kay and myself, too. It's been an unusual holiday. We thought we'd just go off by ourselves and visit Galway and the coast and things like that. Do you know what I mean, Patrick? But then we met you and we've had a brilliant time. We will miss you very much when we go back to England. But, Patrick, we will keep in touch. And you'll visit England one day, Patrick." Paul was genuine in his remark.

"We'll have to make the most of the remaining time. Whenever you have a chance the four of us will go and do something. We'll have fun." Keane said.

"Indeed, Patrick. We have today, even in the rain." Paul said.

Then the interval of silence came. Keane would miss them very much. It's been a long time since he felt he had a friend. Everyone always seems to be leaving, never staying. It deeply saddened Keane. Paul was right, Keane thought. So much has happened. Keane never could have predicted such a wonderful time in meeting Paul and Kay, and of course, Pauline. When things appeared desperate, at their darkest, the light of friendship and belonging pushed the darkness away. At a time when Keane seemed to feel at his loneliest, he became surrounded with true friends.

The journey of Abraham was both a literary and a faith story. To be Abraham was to move as Abraham moved. To have faith was to live faith. Abraham was motion even through famine and deception and unbelief. And life is motion. In movement there is blessing.

Life is the length of the river run.

The car pulled up in front of Foley's Market. Keane jumped out of the driver's seat and went quickly to the door. It was raining harder now. He walked inside the damp market and the bell sounded.

"Hi John-Joe." Keane said.

He hadn't seen much of John Joseph Foley in the market. Usually it was only Pauline and some days the Foley's daughter was with Pauline.

"How are you keepin', Patrick?" John-Joe asked him.

"I'm well, thanks."

"The weather's changin' again. Maybe our spell of the sun is over. I don't know yet." John-Joe said, almost in fear.

"Pauline's here, alright. She's finishin' up now. You can go on back if you'd like, Patrick."

"Thank you."

Keane then disappeared into the cold and damp back room where he found Pauline sweeping up.

"Hi Pauline."

He walked over and kissed her. She held him at her lips a moment longer.

"I've missed you, Pakie. Isn't that funny?" She asked in her quiet voice.

"No. It's lovely. I've missed you, too." He kissed her again on the lips.

"John-Joe said you're finishing up. Does that mean we'll be able to go?" He hoped.

"Yes. It wasn't so busy here. I feel bad for the Foley's. It's supposed to be much busier as it's the summer months now. The hotels aren't so busy, though. Have you come with your car?"

"Yes. We went down to Shannon. Everything went well. Paul and Kay are going home in a few days. Monday morning they'll drive back to Dublin to take the ferry across." He was sad at telling Pauline the news.

"Oh, I see. We will miss them. I know you got along wonderfully with them. I'm sorry, Patrick." She said sadly.

"But, we have today and whatever time is left, please God." Keane said.

"Today will be very special, then. We'll make it so, Pakie." She said lightheartedly.

Keane opened the door of the car for Pauline. The rain was still coming down. He went around to his side and got in. They drove home the way in which Keane usually walked. This was the same road that Paddy had taken Keane the first time to Tullamore. He took the back roads on the rise and fall of the hills. Keane carefully went down those three steep areas on which he climbed and saw the distant, the near, the past and the future.

He turned at the bridge where the Travelers set up their camp.

A few miles away he stopped in front of Pauline's home. Keane loved that the homes had much space and land between them. Keane got out of the car and opened the door for Pauline. He walked her to the front door.

"It's a lovely car. Will you drive down to Kilkee?"

"Maybe you'll drive. How about that, Pauline?" They both laughed.

"If you feel adventurous, Pakie." They laughed again.

"We'll pick you up in a little bit. We'll call you. Take your time." He said.

They embraced at her door and neither wanted to let go of the other. They stood in the rain and it wasn't sure if they knew it or not.

Keane pulled the car in front of Tullamore. When he entered it was quiet. No one was home. He thought about

Maeve taking John to the doctor. There was no note from Maeve. Perhaps he would call later as they traveled.

As Keane came out of his room he heard the front door open. He went quickly to the front room.

"Ready, Patrick?" Paul boomed out enthusiastically.

"Hello Paul, hi Kay. Yes, I'm ready."

"Patrick, would you prefer that I drive. After all I'm used to this style of driving. The roads do get a bit tricky." Paul suggested.

"Oh, that would be fine. I'm looking forward to going. Pauline is getting ready now. I can call her and let her know we're ready."

"Lovely." Paul answered.

Keane called Pauline from the phone in the small room squeezed in between the dining room and the kitchen.

The three of them left Tullamore and drove down the long farmhouse road.

"Let's go the back way, Paul. It's the way I often walk to go to my place up there."

Keane instructed Paul to drive toward the Kilshanny church.

"Turn here, Paul. It's a narrow, dirt road with holes in it. But this ride is beautiful."

Paul drove up the steep, narrow, dirt road. Tullamore rose high in the background. The two dogs were out wandering in front of the barn.

"Oh, wow, Patrick. This is high up. It's brilliant! Kay, look out there across the pastures." Paul said.

"Paul, we've never been this way. It's so lovely." Kay stated as she looked out on the green hues darkened by the clouds and the mist.

When Paul was at the turning point where the road ended and another began, he stopped the car. He noticed what Keane had noticed. The break in the high hedges gave a mystical view of the pastures rising and falling in all of their green softness.

Paul got out of the car and walked over. Kay followed and Keane was behind them. They walked to the hedges and looked out. Paul thought the same as Keane. It did appear that the valley was indeed far below them. It drew a person into this illusion and held them until the view released them and the ground sprang up at the person.

"It's brilliant. Patrick, we've never been up here. Never. We've driven around Kilshanny but not here." Paul said excitedly.

"Look over here." Keane said.

He crossed the bony road to the pastures on the other side. Paul and Kay followed as they walked up a steep path through some hedges and finally stopped.

"Oh my." Kay said slowly.

Paul was silent as he looked out. Keane stood in wonder of it all again.

The pastures spread out in patches of green which rose to one side and fell sharply. Just beyond where the pastures fell the ocean met the land.

They all stood for a moment longer in silence.

"It's absolutely brilliant. What seems different about it, although I don't know if I can put it into words, is the way in which it rises to one side and falls so sharply. The other side just drifts down in all of its softness. It seems to go on forever." Paul said.

"Can you imagine building a home out there? Sometimes the fanners sell off a piece of their land to make ends meet.

"There is so much up here in the hills to find. That's why I love to walk through all of this area." Keane said.

"The houses up here are beautiful, too. They are so well matched with their surroundings." Keane continued.

In the car Keane was pointing out different houses and areas that he had walked through so many times.

"Here is where I spend much of my time."

Paul pulled over on the narrow, bony road and they all got out of the car.

"Oh this is lovely, too. You're right; there is so much up here, Patrick." Kay said.

They all stood on the long, stone wall and looked out. Keane took out his whistle and played his air. They looked at him. Paul and Kay never heard him play. When he was finished they clapped. Keane laughed.

"I didn't mean to give a concert. I come here and play and just look out on the pastures and hills."

"That was brilliant, Patrick. You've really found yourself a home here." Paul said.

When they arrived at Pauline's home she came out the front door. Keane greeted her on the walk. Her hands met his hands in the air and he held them. Her hair rested below her shoulders showing the gentle beauty of her face. He could feel her beauty in his hands, in her touch, the way in which her small fingers searched out his touch.

"You are beautiful, Pauline." Keane said softly.

Moments stand tall in time without moving. It was just two people standing on a walk in front of a house in greeting. But that's if one didn't have vision. Kay saw the magnitude of this moment. She understood that at that precise moment time was still and only the gaze of their eyes held it in place. Paul saw it, too. And once their gaze was broken time moved on.

"We're ready for Kilkee." Patrick said light heartedly.

"Hi Paul. Hello Kay." Pauline spoke softly with a smile.

"You look radiant, Pauline." Paul said.

Kay reached for Pauline's hand and squeezed it. She smiled at her knowingly. Pauline smiled back. Both men missed that moment.

In the car they drove slowly passed some of the homes. They looked over when the hedges broke and saw the rise and fall of the pastures. Keane pointed out some more of the land and what lay behind and hidden.

"Patrick! You know so much of the area. How do you do it? Was it all just from walking?" Paul laughed.

"I only leave the hills to go into town and get supplies. And then I return home to my beloved hills." Keane said with a mock tone of seriousness. But that was almost the truth.

They all laughed at Patrick's description of himself.

"I am the Man from Kilshanny."

Pauline looked at him.

"An Fear as Kilshanny." She said softly in Irish.

"The Man from Kilshanny." Keane said slowly as he looked at Pauline.

Her head fell gently onto his shoulder.

For some time the road followed the sea breaking off from view every so often replacing the sea with pastures and hills that climbed toward the waters. It was a peaceful ride along the rural Ireland coast.

The road sent Keane back to not so long ago when he was all alone. He held Pauline's hand as they sat in the rear seat. She looked out the window with a glance toward Keane every so often.

He thought of Pauline, how she held his heart so gently, acceptingly, caring for him, asking for nothing in return. And the land with all its wonder and beauty that brought him closer and closer to home.

The road followed the sea over hills and through pastures and still following the waters. The road was before Keane as it had been always. He thought of home past and present.

Paul and Kay, Pauline and Patrick walked the quaint, narrow streets of Kilkee. The tiny, ancient village once the home of ruling clans hugged the inlet where the sea crept in and shaped the coast.

They walked along a footpath that lined a park where it met the stretch of white beach. They crossed through the grass and went to the sands where the sea was gentle for that day and the breeze was light.

The sun had broke out as they traveled down the coast line and now it was a mixture of bright blue on sky and water and darkness carried by low clouds that threatened to spread further.

The four of them stood at the ocean admiring the day, the sea, and the newness of their friendship. They stood all four happy and content with this day. Then they moved along the sandy edges of the shore. The beach came to an end halted by large rocks and they stood for a moment.

They all seemed larger than the village. Even at the shore line everything seemed tiny in Kilkee. They looked up at the village spreading its small, quaint buildings up a steep hill.

Everything seemed a white-wash of brightness as they strolled through the village. It was a pleasant place and a pleasant afternoon. The silence was comforting as each matched their thoughts with the surroundings.

At lunch they shared these thoughts. It seemed a timeless place and quiet for a seaside town in midsummer.

"Absolutely lovely place, Pauline. Isn't it?" Paul asked.

"Oh yes, quite lovely. It seems also quite quiet for this time of year."

"I think it would be a wonderful place to stay for a holiday." Kay said.

"Yes, it would. It is quite different." Patrick said.

They sat and ate lunch speaking of the day and what they would do next.

"We've spent many wonderful days and evenings together." Keane went on.

"Wouldn't it be brilliant to live in Ireland, Patrick? Imagine having your home up in those hills of Kilshanny. Then you would really be the man from Kilshanny," Paul said.

"That would be a wonderful event." Keane said.

Kay smiled at Pauline and she smiled in return.

They continued in the car down the coast road. It was darker now from the larger cover of cloud that blew in from the ocean. The mist was heavier and it rose over the ocean in a shroud as they looked on it from the road.

"I don't know what Loophead has to offer but I'm willing to stop and give it a go." Paul said after driving awhile.

"Yes, let's see what it is." Keane said.

When they drove nearer they saw the lighthouse first. The tall stone, cylindrical structure stood high above the grassy Loophead peninsula. The boggy and grassy land jutted out over the rugged sea and then crept back in before jutting out again. The low clouds, black and gray, moved silently with the thick mist that rolled over the high cliffs from the ocean.

The lighthouse was in and out of the blanket of mist that moved close to the wet, grassy ground.

They saw no one at all as they pulled up into the small, gravel lot.

"Should we get out?" Paul asked.

"Yes, let's do get out." Pauline said.

"Lovely, then. Let's get out and see Loophead." Paul said cheerfully.

They heard a piper as they shut the doors to the car. They stood a moment listening.

"What a lovely sound." Pauline said in a low voice.

"An Uillean pipe." Keane said.

"It certainly matches the day, doesn't it?" Paul stated.

They moved from the gravel lot to the wet, boggy and grassy land. They were getting wet from the thick mist that both hung and fell from the air. They walked across the grassy stretch toward the edge. They stood at the cliff and looked out on the white-capped sea rushing toward land. The wind moved them back a step but it wasn't as powerful as at the Cliffs of Moher.

The sound of the pipe, the far-away sound that the uillean pipe pours out, drifted through the wind and the mist. Keane looked up the peninsula to find where the piper was playing.

"Let's go to the piper." Keane offered.

They all walked near the edge of the dramatic cliffs rising from a stormy sea. There were no tourists here. In that regard, Keane better liked Loophead.

"There he is, Pakie." Pauline pointed.

They stopped for a moment to listen to the man's playing.

The piper's folded, white and red cane lay next to him.

The uillean piper played on for his visitors. His far-away notes filled the air and brought them all closer.

"Play your whistle, Pakie. He won't mind at'tall, I promise." Pauline whispered.

Keane took his whistle out of his back pocket and joined the piper in the sweet, slow air.

The piper played with more intensity looking over in Keane's direction with a nod as he worked the bellow. Keane stepped in closer and the two of them were buried in the tune that filled the mist.

"Lovely." The piper said.

"If s a brilliant day for the pipes and the whistle now isn't it?" The piper added.

"It's very fitting. Thank you for playing and thanks for letting me in the tune." Keane said.

"You're quite welcome, I'm sure. Visiting today?" the piper asked.

"Right. We've come down from Ennistymon just driving along the coast. We noticed Loophead on the map." Keane explained.

"If s always empty of people here. Only a few stop by now and again. Everyone fancies the Cliffs of Moher." The piper said with a laugh.

"But I come here often and play to the sea. It's quite challenging having the sea as your audience. It can get quite upset at times. I'm trying to calm it down now. Maybe bring out the sun for a bit."

He paused.

"Join me in a reel?"

"Ready." Keane said.

The piper played a reel quick and fanciful and Keane caught the rhythm with his whistle. The playing got furiously fast and Keane stopped to watch the man play his pipes so brilliantly.

Keane started again and they finished out the reel in a loud fury of sound.

"Look! Look!" Pauline startled everyone. "It's light coming from the distance. You've done it. You've calmed the sea." She laughed.

"Lovely. God bless."

And the piper played his tunes as he sat under his makeshift covering of tarp stretched out on three poles.

The clouds moved swiftly uncovering Loophead from their grip. The sun stretched its light under and through the mist providing a mystical and magical setting.

The wind picked up its strength slightly as it swept the darker clouds away. The sky remained a mixture of lighter clouds and sunlight in the breaking pale blue sky.

Paul and Kay were trailing behind Patrick and Pauline as they walked the grassy peninsula near the cliffs. Pauline grabbed Keane's hat off of his head and ran with it.

"Hey, that's my hat. I love that hat!" Keane shouted in the wind.

Pauline kept running as the wind carried her laughter back to Keane.

He chased her over the wet, slippery ground.

Pauline placed the hat on her head, laughing, and continued her fun as she darted over the wet land.

Paul and Kay were laughing, too, as they watched the fun.

Pauline was running near the edge with the great, dramatic expanse of the cliffs and the sky as the backdrop. Her body, thin and narrow, danced lightly over the great area of grassy land near the high cliffs.

Keane ran faster to catch up with Pauline. He darted quickly toward her in surprise. Pauline lifted off of the ground in flight as her legs moved quickly to get away.

As she ran she turned toward the cliff and the wind caught the wide brim of the hat and lifted it high and lofty off of her head. She screamed as she frantically reached up for the hat which was by now high above her head in a strong draft of wind.

Paul pointed as Kay watched as the hat flew over Pauline. Keane stopped as he saw his Akubra take off over the cliffs. Pauline screamed again as the realization hit everyone at once. Keane's hat would not be coming back. It was caught in the high draft of wind current making the

Akubra soar high and then it was swept over the ocean as it began its fall into the depths of turbulent waters.

They all gathered at the edge and watched the demise of the Akubra as it was dragged down into the white-capped ocean. It was gone now.

"I guess, Patrick, it's gone for good now." Paul said in his cheerful voice.

"Well, it was a dramatic ending for a noble hat such as it was." Keane said with a smile.

"Oh, Patrick! I'm so sorry! Please..." Pauline started to speak.

"Ah! No one liked the hat any way. Don't worry." He laughed.

Then he reached for her waist in a quick moment.

"But now you owe me a hat, Miss O'Sullivan!" He shouted with great laughter.

"We'll see, Mr. Pakie!" Pauline said as she escaped his reach.

Pauline ran off again as Keane chased her over the green, wet ground.

Laughter filled the air along with the sound of the uillean pipe. Paul and Kay watched as the two ran off one chasing the other in great fun.

They arrived back at Tullamore at nine o'clock in the evening. They sat in the front sitting room of the house. Keane walked over to the dining room door getting ready to go in and see Maeve about John. Maeve was on her way out and met Keane by the door of the dining room.

"Well, the tourists are back I see. And how is everyone?" She spoke loudly so everyone could hear as she walked toward them.

"Good evening, Maeve." Paul said as he rose from his chair.

"Please sit, Paul. How is everyone? Pauline?"

"Good evening, Maeve." Pauline spoke softly.

"We had a great day, Maeve." Keane said.

He waited to see if Maeve would mention John.

"We went off to Kilkee and then Loophead. It was lovely." Kay said.

"Kilkee is lovely. John and I have been down there on holiday. We were very pleased with the area." Maeve said.

"Let me tell you." Maeve broke in with a new thought.

"John hadn't been feeling well, as Pakie knows, and I took him today to see the doctor."

Everyone sat straight and attentive.

"He is resting well in the Ennis Hospital. The doctor found a blood clot in his leg. The doctor wants to observe him for a few days to make sure the medicine will work. He's doing fine considering, though. Of course, John doesn't ever do well in hospitals. He likes to be home on his farm."

"I'll go tomorrow to see how he is doing." Keane said.

"Thank you, Pakie. That would be lovely. I know John would love to see ye."

"I'll leave you now and I'll see everyone at breakfast.'Night!" She spoke as she left the front room.

Pauline rose quickly and caught Maeve in the dining room.

"How are you really, Maeve? What can I do for you?"

"It's been a long day. I do feel tired at the moment. I'll be fine, though, Pauline. Thank you, dear."

"Why don't I manage breakfast alone in the morning. You rest." Pauline had her hand on Maeve's arm.

"I think I should just stay busy. After breakfast I'll go see John. I'll see you in the morning, Pauline." She hugged Pauline and left through the kitchen door.

"We'll see you at breakfast, then, Patrick?" Paul asked.

"Eight-thirty." Keane answered.

"Good night, Pauline. Wonderful to spend the day with you." Paul told her.

"Good night, Pauline. Patrick." Kay said.

Keane pulled up in front of Pauline's house and shut the car off. He walked Pauline to her door.

"Do come in, Patrick." Pauline said softly.

They both entered her home and sat in her living room. Pauline came close to Patrick and put her arms around him.

"I've had such a lovely day, Pakie.

"I'm so happy. I can feel how happy I am deep inside of me." She explained with her head leaning into his chest.

"I'm sorry about your hat. We'll get you another."

"Oh, I'm not worried about it. It really took off high and mighty, though, didn't it?" He laughed.

In the morning Keane awoke to the sound of wind and rain. After getting ready for the day he went to grab his hat and stopped suddenly. He grinned at the thought of his hat sailing into the ocean. He left the house early as usual with a jacket on because of the cool rain.

He walked down the long farmhouse drive in the morning rain. The landscape was new from the darker hues of green across the pastures.

He came to the white Kilshanny church and didn't stop at the wrought-iron gate. He opened it and went on into the sanctuary. He walked the aisle up to the front pew and, before going in, he knelt at the pew and gave the sign of the cross.

He prayed thinking of John and Maeve, Paul and Kay, and thinking of Pauline whom he loved.

"Good morning, Patrick." Father Kelly spoke from the door on the other side of the pews.

"Good morning, Father." Keane rose to greet the priest from Galway.

"So many blessings, aren't there, Patrick? So many things for which to be thankful. And it's a blessing to have people for whom you can pray. It gives one a sense of belonging, doesn't it?" He asked but did not wait for the answer.

"Stay well in this rain, Patrick. Please let Maeve know that I'll give John a visit. God bless." And he was gone through the other door.

In the rain Keane turned up the narrow, muddy road past the barn and down into the valley and turned past his place. He walked toward Pauline's home. Father Kelly was right, Keane thought, it all was a blessing.

11

The River Run

Time had harbored what was necessary to shelter and to protect. A cycle of a life offers its moments of immunity. The span of years in which existence is stirred, prompted and provoked, has its periods of containment and release. Time is a liberating force in which one moment to the next a certain freedom is set forth as a reprieve. As even Abraham eventually moved on from under the Terebinth Tree time's elasticity launches life forward. What can be perceived as shelter can often be a hindrance to movement. As liberator time will unbind the static moment and unchain the harbored soul.

Patrick Keane awoke early as was his habit at Tullamore. He sat in the wicker chair facing the bed with his suitcase open. He was packing what he needed to take home. The moment of release was imminent. The past would be let go and life would be a beginning once again. The foreword to the source of life was belonging. Keane would find the ending of his long, cold, lonely past by letting it meet the warm beginning.

Keane put what he needed into one black luggage bag. He closed it and placed it on the other, unused bed. He left his room and headed in the familiar direction of the front sitting room.

Paul and Kay were coming down the stairs as Patrick approached the front room.

"Patrick Keane!" Paul bellowed out.

Keane had never seen the two of them awake or out of their room at this early hour.

"Patrick Keane!" Paul bellowed once again.

"Going for your walk? Going to the church are you?" Paul asked.

"Good morning to the both of you. Yes, I'm out as usual." He attached a small laugh to the comment.

"Mind if we join you? We've never taken the walk before. It's a lovely morning as well, Patrick." Paul stated.

"I would love your company. Please, come for the walk. As I've been telling you, it's a great walk. You'll see all of Ireland now."

Patrick Keane, his friends Paul and Kay Martin walked under the thick branches of the mighty tree that stood protectively on the front pasture of Tullamore Farm House. They walked under the great tree and continued on down the long, winding farmhouse road.

The Terebinth Tree was behind them now. They walked under the clear, open, morning sky. From the high farmhouse road they walked above the bordering hills surrounding the distance like a gate.

"Look at that! I've never noticed it as I drove down this hill." Paul stated.

"Yes, you could easily see it from here." Keane stated.

"It rises in the clearing where the hills seem to lower and clear a way to go." Paul said.

He pointed at the tall spire of the church rising once again out of the soft, green hues of the rising and falling hills.

They followed the narrow, bony road that Keane had by now walked on so many mornings and afternoons.

They ensued the spire of the white Kilshanny church as it rose and then fell back beneath the rising hills only to come out again as guide, beacon, and direction.

At the wrought-iron gate they paused to admire the building. Paul pulled up the metal latch of the gate and opened it wide. They walked into the sanctuary in silence and went to where Pauline guided Patrick.

In prayer the three of them knelt, heads bowed low in hands.

When their prayers were lifted into the unseen they walked over and lit candles. One for protection on Paul and Kay's journey home, one for Keane's journey home, one for Pauline, and one for those in need.

"You lit an extra candle, Patrick." Paul said.

"It's for going home." Keane said it slowly and meaningfully.

Paul and Kay watched his face as he said the words. But they didn't ask him any more about it.

As they approached the narrow, dirt road Paul stopped.

"Shall we get Pauline?"

"Great idea!" Keane exclaimed.

"It's such a wonderful morning. Brilliant! Now I'm realizing why you didn't at first lease a car, Patrick. I've been missing all of this beauty. I'm afraid I've been a tourist where as you've been a resident." He laughed.

"No. You'll never be a tourist, Paul." Keane shook his head.

They walked up the narrow, dirt road as Tullamore stood high to the side of them. They went passed the barn where the dogs were out and the sound of metal and voices were heard.

Then they began their descent into the mystical wonder of the land. The narrow, dirt road fell quickly lifting the pastures on either side up high giving the illusion of walking atop their soft, green covering. The three of them went through the sanctity of the moment.

"What an incredible experience, Patrick. It's absolutely brilliant." Paul bellowed out.

"Pauline and I love walking through here."

Patrick knocked on the door as the three of them stood to welcome Pauline.

Pauline came and opened the door with surprise.

"Paul and Kay! How lovely to see you. You've come to gather me so you could have your breakfast." She laughed softly as she put her hand on Keane's wrist. Her gentle fingers wrapped around not wanting to let go.

"Yes, Pauline. We've come in order to get breakfast. We can't have it any longer unless you serve it to us." Paul laughed.

"Please come in. I'll only be a moment."

They sat in Pauline's living room while she finished getting ready.

Keane got up out of the chair and went to see Pauline. He watched her as she brushed her hair by the mirror.

"Good morning, Patrick." She smiled at him.

"Hi. You look lovely."

"Come here, Pakie."

Keane walked the few steps over and Pauline put her arms around him and gave him a soft kiss on his lips. He held her tightly as he kissed her, too.

"I'm ready now." Pauline whispered as she moved her lips slightly over his mouth.

He stared at her and saw his own life in the deepness of her dark eyes.

"We'll go now. Maeve will be calling for me if I'm not there soon." She spoke and broke the trance.

They walked passed Keane's place, the long, stone wall, and continued on.

"Have you gone to the church this morning?" Pauline asked them as they walked along the bony road.

"Yes, Pauline. We walked there before getting you. We've lit candles for our journeys." Paul said.

"I lit one for my journey home." Keane said.

The three of them looked at him. It was a solemn tone and unusual that Keane would mention going back home now.

"You have a little more time, though, Patrick. Right?" Pauline said in an even tone.

"I have some time remaining before I go back to America, yes. But I am speaking now of my home. I haven't mentioned it to any one yet. It's so deep within me that it's rather difficult to speak about. Although it should be easy as it's a wonderful thing to go home." Keane tried to explain.

They were all looking at him in wonder.

They made the turn up the narrow dirt road. The hill before them rose in all of its wonder as the pastures seemed to hold it up in mid-air. A light rain fell as unexpectedly as Keane's statement.

"I'm going home to Longford." He said it. "It's the place of my birth. I left there with my parents when I was just above two years of age. I have never been back. And I have felt very lost because of it. I need to go home. As you know my parents have died. I don't know what is back there for me. It's such a deep yearning within me."

He was struggling with the words and the meaning.

They were passing through the moment when the pastures met the rise of the hill and all of them were walking atop the pastures in a timeless moment.

Pauline reached for Patrick's hand. This was the silence that she knew was in him. She never asked him about it. She understood that when he was ready to speak he would do so. She knew his honesty and she understood the framework of time in which words often needed to comply.

No one as yet spoke. Paul, Kay, and Pauline waited for Patrick to let out all of that which has been stored in him for all those many years.

"I wanted to come to Clare first, as a sort of resting place. A place to get ready to go further home. I don't know why, but I couldn't just go right to Longford. I needed to journey in stages, as Abraham had done. Maybe for different reasons, but we both needed to take a journey in stages. I've never felt quite complete as a person. I've always been a step away, a distance that has kept me from feeling a sense of belonging to any thing, or anyone. I've been alone all of my life. That has been to my neglect but I never found a way out of it. Even at the seminary I felt a step away, never quite in the middle, never quite a part of it. I would always go in to Loretta at the bookstore and talk with her. I think she understood me. I've loved very much what I've taught but being at the seminary has given me little joy."

His words fell out but not escaping the attention of Paul, Kay, and Pauline.

They walked with him through this moment. Up the hill on the narrow, dirt road they walked together.

No one spoke except Patrick.

"And now I'm going home." He stopped suddenly on the steep hill.

"I have to say, though," he paused and held Pauline's hand tighter.

"I feel as if I'm already home. Pauline, Kay, Paul, you have been so wonderful to me. Even though a short time has gone by, for me the moments have evolved into a strong bind of friendship."

He paused.

"And more." He looked at Pauline.

"So, after a life time of not knowing, I've come here to know and put to rest the past and then move on toward today."

He was finished.

He told them.

He had been holding it in, not just for this time with them, but for all of his life.

They walked down the narrow, dirt road with Tullamore rising in the short distance.

Pauline did not want to speak. She reached around Patrick with both arms and held him tightly resting her head on his chest.

"That's brilliant, Patrick. You've come home." Paul stated.

There weren't many words that would be fitting at this moment.

"County Longford." Paul paused a moment. "I can't quite place where it's located."

"That's the midlands up near Roscommon." Kay explained.

"It's low-lying country with lots of streams and lakes. It's quite beautiful." Kay went on further.

"Yes, that's it, Kay. I only remember the small, white house. And then driving away that day as I sat in the rear seat looking out. I was crying for my bicycle." Keane said.

"Patrick, thank you for telling us. I'm sure it wasn't an easy moment for you. This trip has turned out to be quite meaningful for you; well, it has from the start, I suppose." Paul said.

"It has been meaningful. It's been wonderful. And now that I've said it, I feel released and ready to go the last stage of the journey."

He looked at Paul and Kay.

"I'm going home."

"Patrick, if you don't mind, this calls for a celebration. It's also fitting as Kay and I are leaving for home in the morning. We were supposed to leave this morning but we've changed our plans. The ferry ride over to England would have been very rough for today. We've decided to wait. Let's say we go to Lahinch tonight and have a time of it? What do you say, Patrick?" Paul asked with merriment.

"Perfect. Let's go to Kenny's Pub. We'll sing some songs. Miriam and the kids should be there tonight. Pauline, how does that sound to you?"

"It'll be great fun. It's a grand day, Pakie. A very grand day!"

She felt the release of Patrick's pressure of keeping the story within himself. She knew the loneliness he experienced. It was her loneliness, too. This day marked the beginning.

The four of them walked up the long, winding farmhouse road.

"Why do you think I've waited this long to come home, Pauline?" Patrick asked her as he sat in her living room.

It was later in the day now as they both relaxed in Pauline's home.

Paul and Kay walked along the sandy strip of land above the craggy rocks that kept back the sea. This was there place. Paul held her hand as they walked toward where the sea came in to rest within the enclosing land. The late afternoon brought the quiet of the day. For Paul and Kay, this was their last walk on the beach which had become their place to come and be renewed.

"This is quite a special place, dear." Paul told his wife.

"It's very lovely." She replied.

"It's been quite perfect. We've had our time alone here and we spent some lovely time with Patrick and then with Patrick and Pauline. It's been quite a holiday." He said.

"Yes. It's been very special. I'm happy for us and I'm happy for Pauline. And Patrick is going home." She said quietly.

"That was some story he told us. It must have been very difficult for him. He's kept it in for so long. Why do you think he's waited for so long to come home?" Paul asked.

"Pakie, it just needed to be the right time. It never was right for you until you fully realized that home is where you needed to go. Once you knew it, understood it, and mostly, have accepted it, you've come home. I think it is as simple as that, Patrick.

"Anyway, I'm glad you've waited. If you'd come before, I just might have missed you." She looked into his eyes.

Patrick peered silently back into Pauline's eyes. He didn't say anything. She was right. She understood him.

"I think that Patrick had to wait. Now, when the time was right, he came home. He met Pauline. It all fit so perfectly together. The past no longer matters. Home is always the direction of the heart." Kay said thoughtfully as she held onto her husband's hand.

They walked on the sandy trail the remaining distance back.

Keane pulled into the parking lot near O'Looney's and stopped the car. He came around and let Pauline out, with a kiss. They walked toward the top of the street to Kenny's Pub.

Paul and Kay were already sitting in the narrow, cushioned booth next to Miriam and the two children. There was room enough, and not much more at all, for Pauline and Patrick. They squeezed in and sat down.

"Hello Miriam. Hi Peter and Kathleen." Keane waved to the children sitting in chairs at the end of the short booth with the small round table in front of it.

"Will you join me in some songs tonight, Pakie? It was grand last time. You haven't been here for awhile." Miriam said.

"If you're asking me, I would love to sing some songs tonight."

"That'd be lovely." She said.

Paul ordered a round of pints for the bunch of them and two soft drinks for Peter and Kathleen.

At about half-nine the crowds were already in place at Kenny's.

Miriam started with some well known Irish pub songs with Peter joining in on accordion and Kathleen on the whistle. Everyone who knew the words sang out.

After some time Miriam leaned over to Keane.

"Would you like to get the crowd going?" She laughed.

"I don't know if I can do that, but I'll play some songs, gladly." He joked.

Miriam handed the guitar over to Patrick. Some people remembered him from the last time and they yelled to Keane.

"Pakie, play some Dylan!"

Keane strummed the guitar once and went right into Clare to Here. Keane sang the song with the proper feeling needed to sing that particular sad song.

The crowd loved it and clapped loudly. More than a few were deep into their pints.

He began next with one of his favorites, Wild Colonial Boy, with many joining in wherever they could remember a line or two.

Next was The Rare Old Times.

After a few more of the Irish songs Keane decided on a few American tunes.

"Here's one from the early seventies. It's always been a top one for me."

And he sang a Cat Steven's song, How Can I Tell You.

Keane always thought it was a very beautiful song. And now he felt it was fitting to bring it back for this night.

Everyone fell silent. Keane's voice filled the smoke-filled room. He looked over at Peter and nodded. Peter went into a solo bit during the song. He was only twelve years of age and played the accordion with a good feel. Kathleen joined in the solo with her wooden Irish flute. One man at the bar tipped his pint back and emptied it into his mouth. Another man hugged his girlfriend, or maybe it was his wife.

Keane ended with some great Bob Dylan songs. The Man in Me, Emotionally Yours, Under the Red Sky, Shelter from the Storm, and a rousing version of When the Ship Comes In.

Kenny's Pub was filled with fun, smoke, and the smell of stout. The people came for drink and music and they yelled out for another tune.

Miriam leaned over to Keane and whispered into his ear.

"I don't think you can give the guitar back now, Pakie." And she laughed.

"They're fun but I think they'd be yelling at anyone to continue." Keane laughed, too.

"I'll play this one for my friends, Paul, Kay and Pauline."

As he spoke he spotted Mike and Kathleen Cahill and Ita coming into Kenny's.

"And to the scoundrels who've just entered!"

Everyone looked and laughed.

Kathleen pierced the room with her laughter.

Keane sang another old tune New Horizons by the English band The Moody Blues. A song of hope filled the pub.

Kathleen, Mike, and Ita came over when Keane finished the song. They carried chairs with them and placed them around the small table.

"It's been so long, Patrick!" Kathleen said.

"We loved it the last time you sang here with Miriam. I'm sorry we missed the fun tonight." Kathleen continued.

"Hello, Pakie!" Mike yelled out.

Everyone greeted each other and spoke of the other nights they shared at Galvin's and Kenny's.

The night went on filled with pints and laughter. Keane sang more songs and Pauline, too, sang some songs. At one point a gentleman of eighty-one, as he let everyone know, took out his whistle and played two jigs and a reel that brought the pub to a stomping, roaring thunder.

When the evening was at an end Kathleen managed to come close to Keane.

"We've missed you!" She said.

"We all had such fun. Thank you. Pauline and I have been doing things together. We haven't come often to Lahinch."

"Oh, so it's love that's got you. Lovely!" She laughed the way Keane remembered.

"You were doing very well this evening, Pakie." Larkin said to him from his car as the four of them walked passed him in the parking lot.

"Thank you, Larkin. I enjoyed myself very much."

"Good night, everyone! Bye Pakie!" Kathleen, Mike, and Ita yelled out from across the street.

The night was over and the pub would close soon. It always took a while to empty everyone out. Paul, Kay, Pauline, and Patrick walked slowly to their cars which were parked in the same lot.

The ocean breeze blew into the night. Paul looked out into the darkness. He saw the empty and undisturbed sandy path nearby.

Patrick followed Paul back to the farmhouse road and then went on further beeping the horn as he passed them.

The new day brought the mist coming from over the nearby ocean. It covered the land as a veil just rising above the face of the land but hanging lightly as it reached for the ground.

Patrick entered the church and went to the front. As he knelt in prayer Pauline slid in beside him touching his arm as she knelt.

Through devotion things are given for which have never been asked. The two of them knelt in their devotion taking the moment to appreciate what is present in their lives.

Afterwards, they lit a candle. They put the small flame to one single candle for Kay and Paul.

"Good morning, Miss O'Sullivan. Good morning, Mr. Keane." Father Kelly came out through the door once again.

He came over and touched both of their shoulders.

"What has been added to your lives is much. It's a wonderful blessing to see. When do you go home, Patrick?" Father Kelly looked at Keane.

"I leave in about two weeks. But first I'm making a stop in Longford. It's where I was born. I haven't been back since I left as a child."

"I see, I see." Father Kelly said while rubbing his chin.

"Then in many ways you've come home. It is the great story, isn't it? Abraham on his journey back by going forward." He let his words fill the space Keane had left.

"Good morning to the both of you. Let me know, Patrick, how your trip turns out. God bless." And he left through the other door.

"He's a good man, Pakie." Pauline said as they walked out of the sanctuary.

"Thank you for coming this morning."

Keane held her hand.

They walked through the wrought-iron gate and turned toward Tullamore.

"I thought you'd be here at this hour. So I've come to be with you. You needn't walk alone. How about the cliffs today, Pakie? After we see Kay and Paul off. It'll help settle our sadness a bit to be there looking out over the ocean standing in the wind feeling the power of the earth."

"Yes, that would do us well to be there. I would love it. We'll go as soon as you're off from Maeve's. Oh, but what about Foley's today?" Keane asked.

"There is no work there today, so I'm free this afternoon."

Together they walked up the long farmhouse drive. Keane went into his room and Pauline disappeared into the kitchen. Guests were coming out of their rooms getting ready for breakfast. Paul and Kay were not yet out of their room.

Pauline came and knocked on Keane's door even though it was open wide.

"Pakie, Maeve's asking for you. Breakfast is up."

"Oh, thanks, Pauline. I'm coming."

"Where would you be eating this morning? Would you like a place set with Paul and Kay?"

"Yes, please. That would be wonderful."

He followed Pauline out of the room and as he was stepping into the dining room he saw Paul carrying luggage through the front door. Keane hurried over to the front room giving a yell to Paul.

"Let me help you, Paul. Here."

He grabbed one piece of luggage. Together they walked to the car.

"Thank you, Patrick. We don't have much, really."

Neither man mentioned good-bye or leaving. Neither man wanted to identify with the moment that hung down as the mist which was suspended heavily over the ground.

"Whatever there is I'm glad to help."

He handed Paul the luggage bag and he put it into the trunk of his car.

They made one more trip to the car carrying more bags.

"Alright." Keane said, as he grabbed two bags.

"I hope you don't mind I've invited myself to your table this morning."

"The invitation has always been there, Patrick."

His friends were leaving and Keane was saddened by good-bye. He stood outside peering into the mist. It provided no answers for Keane. They both stood and probed into the low-lying cloud. The silence was as the mist suspended in the air above the ground.

"One more, Paul." Kay yelled out as she carried another bag down the walk to the car.

"Thanks, dear." Paul took the bag and placed it in the trunk with the other bags.

The three of them stood out in the shrouded morning. There was only one thing clear. This was the morning for good-bye. Whether spoken or not at this moment it was good-bye. And it was sad.

Pauline came out and walked down to the three of them.

"We're going to meet again and it will be soon as well." Pauline's voice cut through the mist clearing a path for brightness.

This was one time, yesterday was another time, and another time lies in the future. There is containment and then release. There is shelter and there is the unbinding.

"Let's all meet at Christmas time. That would make the holidays so grand." Pauline continued letting hope rise to the surface.

"Pauline that's a smashing idea. I think we can manage that. Kay? Do you think we can manage a holiday at Christmas time?" Paul was ever enthusiastic.

"That would be so lovely. We should all meet back here in Kilshanny at Christmastime, please God." Kay said.

"Then it's settled. We shall all meet for the holidays. My house is open to everyone." Pauline's face carried a broad smile without a burden.

They walked inside and sat at the familiar table.

Pauline hurried inside the kitchen grabbing plates that Maeve was handing her. She hurried back into the dining room carrying plates.

Keane went inside the kitchen.

"Good morning, Maeve. Let me help with my table. I can take the plates and whatever is ready to go."

Maeve was moving quickly through the kitchen. The smell of all the different foods filled the room.

"Good morning, Pakie. Your friends are leaving today, Mr. Pakie." Maeve said as she put slices of toast in a basket for Pauline to take out to the dining room.

"Yes. I'm going to miss them very much." Keane said sadly.

"Tea or coffee, Pakie?" She asked.

"Tea for Paul and Kay and coffee for myself, please."

In a few moments Keane carried the tea out to Paul and Kay returning in another moment with his coffee.

After breakfast Paul, Kay, Pauline, and Patrick gathered outside in the clearing mist.

Pauline had just managed to finish up with the guests and took a moment to say goodbye.

"Bye Paul. Bye Kay."

Pauline went to first Paul and then Kay and gave each a hug.

"It's been quite a time, Patrick. It was absolutely brilliant. This may have been the best holiday I've ever been on. The weather was clear for the most part, the area is splendid and Tullamore is a wonderful place to stay. But it was all topped with your friendship, Patrick. And yours, Pauline. You are our friends and we shall never forget you. We'll call you, Patrick, when you return back to America. Let us know everything, will you?" He was looking around him.

First he looked at Patrick, then Pauline, then the ground and finally at his wife. His face changed to a strained hopeful look. He was struggling with goodbye.

Keane stepped in closer to Paul and reached out with his hand.

"Good-bye, Paul." He shook his hand firmly.

"Thank you for your friendship."

"Have a safe trip home. God bless." Keane continued.

"Kay, thank you. We're going to miss you very much. We will speak together soon. God bless." He said to her. He shook her hand, too.

All the good-byes were said and they hung in the air as the mist had done earlier. The only clearing would be to drive down the long, winding farmhouse road.

"Paul! Kay!" Maeve bellowed from the front door.

"Just one more good-bye!" She yelled as she came down the walk.

"Good-bye to the both of you. Pleas have a safe journey home. Thank you for staying with us. God bless."

She had enjoyed their company very much.

The clearing came. They drove down the long farmhouse road. Keane watched with deep sadness as the car disappeared into the valley. But he stayed moments longer. He saw them drive by on the narrow, bony road below where the hedges broke for a clearing.

Something emptied out of Keane as the car drove away. He looked at Pauline. She was staring at him. She stepped in closer and took his hand.

"let's go to the cliffs, Pakie." That's all she said and it was enough.

Back in his room Keane was getting some things ready for his trip to Longford.

"Pakie?" Maeve spoke with her strong voice at Keane's door. She came to see if he was well.

"Maeve. I have to tell you I'll be going for a day or so but coming back." He looked at her.

"Would you be needing better directions to Longford, Pakie?" She looked at him with a slanted smile.

Keane looked at her with confusion. Although he knew he shouldn't have been surprised.

"How did you know?" He said finally.

"Pakie. It is I who straightens out your room when Pauline is doing other things. You had three maps of Longford spread out for the world to see. And a large black circle around Kilashee." She laughed with him.

"Oh, I see." He shrugged his shoulders.

Maeve didn't ask about the trip. But Keane wanted to tell her.

"Oh, Pakie. I knew you had something inside of you while you were here. No one really travels alone as you've done. Have you any family present in Kilashee?"

"I don't know. It was a long time ago. I know there was family one time. But I didn't go then. I remember my Uncle Thomas drove myself and my parents on the day we left. I want to go to where I was born."

"Ok, Pakie. let me know if you need anything." She said with gentleness. She had been sitting next to him on the bed.

Pauline and Keane stood at the cliffs. The wind was very strong coming off of the ocean. The wind felt good at the moment. They sat in Pauline's place which overlooks the rushing sea. They sat close with Keane's arm around

Pauline. Pauline was always right. It was the place to be at the moment. The wind blew strong, the ocean roared with force at the cliffs which never moved.

12

In Kilashee

Paul and Kay were home in England now. They stepped back into their familiar brick and stone village surroundings once again. Although they had not been away from home for a long period of time Kilshanny had proposed a design for their near future.

Home could mean different things at separate times. Life is a rhythm in which living is the motif.

Paul thought more about Kilshanny upon his return to England. The cadence of the not-too-distant rhythm called Kilshanny became a flux of ebb and flow within him.

On a day when the ebb and flow of that memory drew on Paul he went into a music shop looking for the song Keane had sung on that last night in Kenny's Pub. He found the recording of New Horizons and purchased it.

That evening Kay came in and found Paul sitting in the family room looking out the window with this song playing.

"I've been thinking, dear." Paul said.

"Yes, I see you have. This is the song Patrick sang that evening. It's very lovely."

"I've been thinking of home. Isn't that silly." He looked at her with a half smile with some embarrassment for sounding so whimsical.

"Kilshanny is a lovely place. It's not silly at all. And we've discussed retirement. I think it is a distinct possibility of considering Kilshanny. After all, I've been away from home, Dublin, for all these many years. Maybe it will do me well to go back." She knew his thoughts and shared his sentiments.

Keane parked his car in front of Pauline's home. After walking to the church earlier he took his black luggage bag packed for a short trip and drove to Pauline's home.

"Good morning, Pakie." She said with a delicate smile.

"Are you alright?" That was the question in her eyes. It was the question she spoke out loud.

Pauline brushed her hand in a motion indicating entrance into her home.

"I'm fine. It's kind of exciting which keeps me ready for the trip. I was more nervous about it when I didn't speak it to you but now I've said it and I'm ready. I'm glad you know."

"I'm glad you've told me. Do you need anything? I mean," she looked away and back again in a quick motion,

"Do you want me to go with you? It may be difficult for you to return alone."

It would be best if she went with Keane she thought to herself.

"I think I'll make the last stage as I've made the first of it. But thank you. Just knowing you care gives me the strength. Anyway," he brushed his hand in the air,

"I'm just going home. If I can call it that name. It's just home. People go home everyday." He said it but he didn't believe it.

"Not after some forty years, Patrick. Not when they've been searching for so long. This isn't coming home from a day's work. It's coming home from a lifetime." No more words she thought.

She moved to him and gave him what he needed. She embraced him.

"Come back, Pakie." She said what she needed. She said it to him as she embraced him. She said it to him in a whisper, in a moment of hope.

"Come back."

The car disappeared from Pauline's view as Keane drove down the bony road. He turned onto the road going north.

He was heading for Kilashee. The place of his birth. He was going to the midlands of Ireland to County Longford. The low-lying land of lakes and streams.

Keane felt great to be driving again. The feel of the road underneath him as he gripped the wheel made the journey come alive. The hills passing by in view, the rise and fall of them now in the distance, the absence of them, rushed by his window.

It was odd to Keane that he did very little reflecting on going back to America. There was no reflection on the seminary or anything related.

Every thought seemed to travel between Kilshanny and Kilashee. The power of movement, like holding a hammer heavy to cast impressions into stone, chisels the unnecessary images away to forge the newer moment.

Every thought was a landscape softly brushed. Each perception of Kilashee filled out the portrait. The landscape grew wide in his mind.

The significance was home. Home was Kilashee. But loose and fragmented images of Kilshanny were still present on this new landscape.

He was miles north of Tullamore. The Terebinth Tree was behind him now.

He saw Pauline dancing on the long, stone wall over the image of a deeper valley. She danced as he played. Laughter filled the air.

He thought of the small, white house of decades ago.

He thought of Paul and Kay walking on the beach at Lahinch in a peaceful time. They were finding their own way making more than a holiday as their days were shaping into a design that would come.

He saw himself walking on that narrow, bony road in Kilshanny. It was on an afternoon with the arced sunlight bending over brightened green pastures that Keane heard a child running toward him.

"The sheep are out." The scream came.

"The sheep mister. The sheep are out."

The young boy was all alert as he screamed the announcement of the run-away sheep. It was a big moment for the boy.

The road lifted and Keane indeed did see the herd of escaped sheep coming up the narrow, bony road. There must have been about fifty of them. Keane found a stick in the hedges and walked slowly toward the frightened sheep.

"Ya! Ya! Come on!" Keane was saying to them. He didn't know the exact sheep call and was laughing at himself while he gave out more "Ya's."

But he did it, though. He brought the sheep home.

Now Keane laughed at that memory. It was special to him. This type of thing had happened more times as well.

Keane came upon a fanner moving his dairy cows down the narrow, bony road. Keane looked and saw over twenty-five cows coming at him. He stopped and realized he had two choices. Walk through the cows, right in the middle of them, or climb over the hedges and get in the pasture. Keane started climbing the hedges. The farmer came by at that point and, while laughing at Keane climbing the hedges, told him to just let the cows pass.

"They're more afraid of you now, believe me. No need to jump." He laughed.

Keane laughed at that memory, too. All the moments now formed the man that drove the car to Kilashee. And all the moments revolved around the one Pauline.

He thought of the first moment seeing her. She knocked so softly, so gently, upon his door that morning.

His thoughts turned to when John O'Connor was lying in the hospital bed that time and Keane and Pauline with Paul and Kay came in and had a laugh with him.

They all stayed for the afternoon with John.

Ballymahon seemed wrong. The directions from Maeve seemed like a good idea at this point. He should've used them. He didn't remember Ballymahon being on the way to Kilashee. He kept driving until he came upon a place to ask for new directions.

"Can you help me?"

"Yes, sir. Where are you going?"

"I'm going home."

Keane smiled when he said it. The man gave a short laugh back at Keane.

"Isn't home the other way?" The man asked.

Keane thought about it.

"No. It's in Kilashee."

"You're a bit out of the way but we'll get you there alright. Take the next road which will bring you into Lanesborough. Head northeast at Lanesborough. Kilashee will be right in your path. The road to Lanesborough is a long one. Not much in between mind you. But you'll get there soon enough." The man stepped away from Keane's car.

"Good luck." He started to walk back into the small store.

"Thank you." Keane said as he pulled away.

He thought about that day. He thought about that bicycle. That last ride down the hill before being called into the car filled his mind. His parents, Bill and Maura, standing at the door of the small, white house filled his mind. The picture of Bill and Maura holding each other, dancing, yet looking away filled his mind, too.

The hammer held heavy was casting these impressions into stone.

He thought about his parents. "I miss them." There's never a year or a day that they go away.

Lanesborough.

Keane read the sign with some apprehension. He had to go now. He had to go to Kilashee now. The answers to whatever questions Keane had lie straight ahead.

Kilashee.

He was home. He was born here in Kilashee. He pulled over and sat for a moment. He looked around him through the car window. He drove slowly on.

He had heard enough about Kilashee before his parents died that he just might find his way now. There was the church. Straight ahead then, he thought.

He drove for a few miles and stopped. He remembered from the stories that this was home. This was home. He drove ahead slowly. No need to hurry. No one was pushing him on. He peered out the window and breathed in the air of home.

The car climbed up one of the few steep hills in all of Kilashee stopping at the top. He saw himself on the

small, black bicycle taking those rides down at full speed.
He got out of the car and looked down the hill.

He looked for a long time.

The small, white house stood at the bottom of the
steep hill waiting for him as it had always done when he
was a child on the small, black bicycle. Keane continued to
stare. He couldn't move. The waves of memory rushed in
holding him in place on that hill.

Keane's childhood experiences reached out to him. He
stood a long time. He was gripped by memory. Now he stood,
a man, where he had left as a boy.

Keane turned the car off and let it coast silently
down the hill. A world went by him as the car carried him
down. He stopped in front of his home.

Nothing had destroyed it. Nothing had changed it. He
looked from the window of the car at the small, white
house. He breathed in deeply and opened the car door.

When he got out he looked around him. He finally took
a step forward and walked toward the front door.

He knocked on the door. Keane's hand was shaking
slightly. The door opened and she stood looking at him.
Keane felt his heart compress when he saw her.

"Hello." Keane began.

She wasn't surprised he was an American. At that moment before he spoke she had hoped he was an American.

The moment moved quickly.

"My name is Patrick..."

"Keane." She finished his sentence.

He stared at her not knowing what to say.

"Patrick. I'm Maura's niece. I'm named after your mum. Her sister Kat'leen's daughter. I knew it was you as you are an image of your dad."

She had tears in her eyes. She was crying.

"Please, Patrick. Come in. Come in." She moved her hand with a gentle wave for him to enter.

When he did so she embraced him as tears streamed down her face spilling onto his shirt. He held her tightly in return and tears came down his cheeks, too. And he cried. He was home from the battles of loneliness, home from the war raged in his soul between conquest and surrender to the isolation that held him captive. He was home from all the wondering, home from all the questions. And Maura was there present as a visible angel. She was the image of Keane's mother. It was a dream, it was real, it was both at the same time. And he held this dream tightly. As tight as he has always held onto it.

Standing before him, clutching him, was his family.

It was over, he thought as he held onto Maura. The years of wondering had ended. He held her now not just out of love but also to be certain this moment would never leave again.

Maura looked up at her cousin.

"We've often spoken of you, Patrick. We've often wondered of your whereabouts. You've been so long without your mum and dad. You've been so long without any relations."

She parted from his arms as she spoke.

"Please sit down, Patrick. From where have you come? When did you get here? I want to hear everything. The love we have for your mum and dad has never left us. We've never met but I feel as if I do know you."

"I've been in County Clare for some weeks now. In a place called Ennistymon. There is a part of Ennistymon that I'm staying in called Kilshanny. The time was right to come and see."

"I know Ennistymon. Lovely. With whom are you staying?"

"I'm staying at a Bed & Breakfast. Tullamore Farmhouse. I've met some lovely people, Maura."

"Oh that's lovely, Patrick. Just lovely. Tell me a little bit about yourself whilst I make us some hot tea."

She stood and walked to the kitchen. Keane followed her.

He looked around as they both walked to the kitchen. Here he was brought into the world. This is where it all began for Keane. He looked at what he could as they went to the kitchen.

"You can have a look after tea, Patrick. We need to calm ourselves. We've had quite a shock. After all these years, after all these years."

She began to get the tea ready.

Keane started to speak about himself.

"I've never married. I've had an unsettling time of it. It's been very difficult at times."

Maura looked at Keane, shaking her head as she got the tea ready.

"I never felt settled enough to marry. It wouldn't have been fair to whomever I married. It's been quite lonely and desperate.

"For the last eleven years I had been teaching at a seminary. I received my doctorate degree in Old Testament. I have enjoyed it very much. Before that I wandered around more or less. Searching, looking, hiding. Mostly hiding. Hiding from what I could not tell you. Maybe hiding from this moment."

He went on with his story as she placed the hot tea on the table.

They both sat at the kitchen table. She reached for his hand holding it gently for a moment.

"You're home now. I'm your family."

"I'm married with two sons. They're all up in Longford town working at the moment. We have a shop in Longford. You'll meet them soon. You'll stay for dinner. And you'll stay for the night as well, Patrick Keane. I won't take no for an answer. Tomorrow is another day.

"Your mum's sister, Kat'leen, my mum, is ill at the moment. She's in the hospital. She stays with us. She is frail at the moment. She will be so encouraged to know you are home. Oh Patrick!" Maura sighed and wiped away a tear.

"I'm named after your mum, as I said. We are always speaking about your parents. For us, they never left. Oh, and who'll want to see you is Father Keane. Uncle Tommy Keane. He's your dad's brother. He's retired now. He will be thrilled to the point of bursting to know you've come home."

The shock was transforming naturally into joy.

"I remember him. He drove me and my dad and mom to the ship. "Abraham journeyed in stages,' he told my father as we drove away. I remember sitting there wondering about this Abraham. As it turned out, that's what my dissertation was on. But I remember him. How old is he now? He must be about seventy-five." Keane then took a sip of tea.

"I didn't know if he was still living." He looked at Maura.

"Seventy-six, Patrick. You haven't forgotten, either, that's grand." She said and smiled.

They both sipped tea and looked at one another.

"You're a handsome man as was your dad." Maura smiled.

"With hope and good fortune you'll settle down, Patrick. I think that now you may be ready." She said as she looked into his eyes.

"There is a woman I've met, she is so special, so lovely, Maura. Her name is Pauline. I've met her in Kilshanny. I've had a wonderful time with her." He smiled.

"Oh, have you now, Patrick? That is grand. I'm so happy. You'll have to bring her 'round and we'll meet her. When do you go back to America?"

"I leave in about two weeks."

"Then you'll bring her here in a day or two." She cut him off.

"She should be with you now, Patrick."

"She did want to come with me."

"We'll all have a lovely time." She said smiling.

Maura was beautiful, Keane thought. As was his mother. She looked so much like her. He finished his tea and she poured him another cup. She brought some scones and brown bread to the table.

"Now."

She placed them on the table.

"Eat, Patrick. When the men've come home we'll have a big dinner. If you need anything more to eat presently, please let me know. Help yourself to the bread, please."

She pushed the plate closer. He sipped the hot tea.

"So much has happened in such a short time, Maura. When can I meet Aunt Kathleen? And when can I meet Uncle Tommy?" He asked excitedly.

"We'll visit tonight, sure, Patrick. We'll ring mum soon and tell the good news. As for Uncle Tommy, we'll ring him also and see where he is tonight."

They finished their tea and Keane finished the scones and half of the brown bread. She laughed with a high-pitched giggle. Keane knew that laugh, too.

"Would you like to see your home, Patrick?" She asked knowing the answer.

Keane rose before the sentence was finished.

"Now."

"First, I have something to show you. Come."

She took his hand and led him to the back and down a short flight of steps to a small room filled with boxes and all matter of home storage.

Maura turned on the dim light. But Keane didn't need any brighter light. He saw it immediately.

His small, black bicycle leaned by itself against the wall. Keane saw the picture of it flash like light and heat in his head and heart. He was riding it down the hill. The image was replaying over and over in his mind.

He walked over to it and touched it. His hand slowly went over the metal bars and over the frame. He touched the seat. He saw his father hand him the bike that day when he first got it. Keane had tears in his eyes. Everything within him came flooding out. Everything that stayed so still within him all of these many years now rose to the surface.

"I've missed them so much. I've missed them so much. And I've needed them so much. So many times I turned to them for help even though I knew they were gone. But still I turned."

Maura came over to him and held him.

"It's over now, Patrick. No more crying, Patrick. No more tears. It's all to rest, now." She held him tightly.

"I never would have guessed this bike would still be here." He wiped away his tears with his sleeve.

"I didn't even know if this house would still be standing."

"Let's go up for now, Patrick. The bicycle is safe. As you are." She led him back up the steps.

Through an open window he saw the back yard. He asked to go outside.

"Of course."

He saw the tree still standing. It grew to a great height.

"When we pulled away that day my bike was leaning on this tree. It was a very small tree then, of course. And as we pulled away the wind came and knocked my bike down. I wanted to run and pick it up. The bike was just laying there and I knew, somehow, I would never see it again. Not knowing about today at all."

He stood there admiring the tree, remembering.

"Your Uncle Tommy likes to visit and take care of the tree. It helps him, too."

Maura took Patrick through the rest of the house. Keane had some memory of some things. But in every step he saw his mother and father. In every step he saw their lives. Everything came back that he knew and things came back that he didn't know. He saw them now as he never had the chance to see them.

Keane suddenly felt very tired. The emotions drained him.

"Come sit down, Patrick. You look exhausted. Come."

She brought him back to the living room and they sat down.

"Sit and relax. This has been enough excitement for the day now, Patrick. The men will be home soon and we'll have some dinner."

Patrick rested in the house where he was born. He stretched his legs out as he sat. He looked at Maura while she sat in a chair near him. He saw his mother knitting. He watched her laugh. He heard her voice speaking to him. It was comforting.

"Can I get you something, Patrick?"

Her face held a soft smile which said everything to Keane.

"Maura, I look at you as a Keane but what is your married name?" He said curiously.

"'Tis Noonan. My husband has people in Roscommon. His dad was born in Roscommon."

"Oh, I see. Noonan."

Keane smiled at Maura. She giggled in a short, low sound. She was as gracious as he remembered his mother to be.

As he sat he let his thoughts drift to different and separate areas. Each thought passed with warmth and comfort. It could have been any other way but it wasn't. Time had gone on but with mercy. Some things remained that could have been gone, too. Here now he sat with Maura. She was the daughter of his mother's sister. The house of Keane's people. It still held his people. Now it held him, too, once again.

"I think I'll ring mum. She'll be so excited. This is such news now." Maura stood and walked to the telephone.

Keane heard her at the phone. There was silence and then Maura's melodic voice spoke.

"Hello mum. How are you keepin' today?" She started.

A pause came from Maura to gather the news of Kathleen's health.

"Mum, I have such news for you.'Tis a miracle I tell you. He came today from America. Yes. Patrick Keane, mum. He's well and handsome. Yes, mum."

Keane heard Maura start to cry as she spoke.

"Yes, mum. Hold on." She paused and called out Keane's name.

"Patrick Keane. Mum would love to speak with you."

Keane rose immediately and went to the phone.

"Hello. This is Patrick." Keane started with some nervousness.

"Yes, Aunt Kathleen. I'm doing well. It's so wonderful to be home I couldn't tell you. Yes, I'll be there and tell you all about myself."

"You sound like your father, Patrick. You do. And you'll have to see your Uncle Tommy, of course. Your father's brother." Aunt Kathleen said.

"Yes, I remember him Aunt Kathleen." Keane wiped a silent tear from his eye.

Kathleen spoke for a moment more before Keane said goodbye.

"She's asking for you to come, of course. She wanted to know everything at the moment." Maura laughed.

"So, she's feeling better and stronger and this news has lifted her spirits." Maura continued.

After some time the men came home from Longford Town. Michael Noonan came through the door first. He was Maura's husband. Maura met him quickly at the door when she heard the car pull up. She kissed him hello and called for Keane.

"Patrick Keane!" She gave a yell to him.

"Michael, this is Patrick Keane. Mum's nephew."

"Don't think I don't know him, now." Mike said with good humor and a big smile.

"Patrick! We've heard about you for a long time now. And I recognize you as a Keane anyway." He grabbed Keane's hand and shook it firmly.

He had seen a car outside. There was no surprise that someone was at his home. When he heard the name he knew immediately.

"These are our two boys, Patrick." Maura said as she gathered her sons coming through the door.

"This is Michael Jr. And here is Tommy. Boys, this is my cousin Patrick Keane from America. Mum's sister's boy."

"Hello..." They both said it but both were uncertain as to what to call him.

"I'm confused, too." Keane said.

"Call me Pat, please. That's best." He laughed.

"Alright, Pat. Welcome back." They both said and came into the house.

"Get ready for dinner boys." She told her sons.

"Dinner will be ready soon, dear." She said to Michael.

The three of them sat in the living room. Keane spoke of himself and outlined his life. They spoke of his parents, the house and Michael spoke of himself. He was a gregarious fellow with a welcoming smile and a good sense of humor.

After dinner the boys, Michael, Maura and Patrick went to see Kathleen. Kathleen's husband, John Lynch, had died a few years ago. She was ailing now from a heart condition but seemed to be getting stronger.

They walked down the corridor of the Branch Hospital where Kathleen was resting. They walked into her room.

Kathleen was sitting up in bed. She started to cry as soon as she saw Keane.

"Come here, son." She said.

Keane walked over and hugged her and kissed her warmly on her cheek. She kissed him back a few times with such gladness.

"You're home now, son. You're home now. I am filled with happiness that I have this chance to see you again."

Keane sat on the edge of the bed close to her as he held her small hand.

Michael jr. and Tommy each went up to Kathleen.

"Hi grandma." They said each with a kiss for her.

"Hello, mum." Michael said also with a kiss.

"Mum." And a kiss from Maura.

"I've missed your mum so very much. As I'm sure you have, Patrick. She was a dear sister. And your father. He suffered at her death." Kathleen wept.

It was all like the sea coming up against the shore. The water pushing and drawing back, pushing and drawing back. Each time bringing something new and taking something away. Memories and love, washing up against their hearts, exchanging both.

Keane sat for some time with Kathleen. They spoke for a long time about the house and all the memories. Kathleen filled in all the empty spaces within Keane's life. The river flowed with both beginning and end. Everything was complete now.

Life is the length of the river run.

The nurse came to tell everyone that Kathleen needed her rest. They could come back tomorrow. And Keane would return, too.

On the way back to the house they passed the Kilashee church.

"There's Uncle Tommy's car. He's inside. Would you like to go in, Patrick?" Maura asked.

"Oh yes, I would love that. Thank you."

"Dear," Maura said to Michael.

"Will you drop us off and then take the boys home. Patrick and I will go in."

"Alright, love. Patrick? Are you alright?"

He knew this was exhausting Keane with so much emotion being stirred.

"I'm fine. It's overwhelming but I've waited a lifetime for this moment."

Maura and Patrick got out of the car and walked up the short steps of the church. No one was inside.

Father Keane came to church and prayed and gave Mass for himself. He was retired now but still celebrated Mass for himself and once in a while for the parish.

Father Keane was at the alter finishing Mass. He looked up and momentarily froze.

Coming down the aisle was Maura and Patrick.

Father Thomas Keane, brother of Billy Keane, saw Maura and Billy walking down the aisle. He looked with disbelief.

Father Keane walked down from the alter to greet them.

"Maura!" Father Keane exclaimed.

"And this must be Patrick Keane from America."

He paused.

"Patrick! Welcome home, son." He put his arms around Keane.

Keane's uncle was a short man, narrow, with white hair.

Father Keane looked at his nephew. His hands were upon Keane's shoulder.

"When I saw the two of you coming I saw your mum and dad, son. And then I knew it must be you. We often speak of you. I have always prayed for you.

"Come with me." He said as he grabbed both Maura's hand and Keane's hand.

He led them into the parish office to sit down.

"Please sit. Maura. Patrick.

"Tell me of yourself, Patrick."

And Keane told the story. And Uncle Tommy Keane listened.

As Patrick Keane told his story Father Thomas Keane reached for his long, black pipe. He smacked it a few times against the palm of his hand. He lit it and sat back watching the bluish-white smoke rise and listening to Keane.

When it was all said Father Keane sat for another moment's silence as a small cloud of the bluish-white smoke formed above his head.

"Then you've come to Canaan, then. Abraham journeyed in stages which is all of our lives. The spiritual call back home. You've heard it and responded. That is my favorite reading. The cycle of Abraham."

"This day I give to you this land."

"And the land was between two great rivers. Rivers provide for life. Life is the length of the river run."

Father Keane spoke the words that Keane remembered so well.

Father Keane had always said those words. "Life is the length of the river run."

Keane held back the tears with force. That phrase was an echo that resonated in his very spirit.

Life is the length of the river run.

13

A Sense of Wonder

Father Thomas Keane smoked his pipe as he marked his steps with an even pace. His thick white hair sat disheveled on his head. He walked every morning and evening as a meditation accompanied by a small cloud of bluish-white smoke from his long, black pipe.

Patrick Thomas Keane breathed in the bluish-white smoke as he walked with his father's brother. The morning held a mist in place as they walked together. They had been in silence for some time. Father Keane loved the silence as he walked. Patrick let the silence enfold them as the mist enclosed the morning.

Keane had spent the night with Maura and her family. After breakfast he came here to the Parish church to meet his uncle.

"Would you like to go there now, Patrick? It must have a grip on you like the mist has the morning. It's not far from our steps now."

The silence lifted slightly.

"Yes, Uncle Thomas. I have been thinking of it."

"Fine. And call me Uncle Tommy. I prefer it."

He smiled at Keane and pointed as they continued their walk.

"It's just over there, up ahead."

He walked Keane to a gate and stopped as he pointed again.

"It's the seventh one down straight ahead. Go on yourself, Patrick. I'll wait for ye here." He nudged Patrick on through the gate.

Keane walked on passed other headstones of people who had belonged to the parish. He stopped and looked down at the one in which he came to see.

Father Thomas Keane had his brother and sister-in-law brought back to be buried in the parish they knew so well. It was their land and he didn't want his family to be alone.

Keane knelt down and read the headstone. "William Patrick Keane His Beloved Wife Maura O'Boyle Keane"

He stared at their names for some time. He saw them in the house. He watched them move in images through his younger years. He saw them that day when they all left the small, white house. He saw the two figures embracing in black and white yearning for something of which Keane did not know. He spoke in a whisper.

"I miss you, mom. You've never left me. You have been with me everyday. I want to tell you that I love you. I love you."

He tried to speak more but tears came down.

"And dad, dad...I need you so much. I've made so many mistakes without your guidance. I have needed you so very much. Please know how much I love you."

Keane placed his shaking hand on the headstone. His fingers traced William's name and then slid slowly down to Maura's name.

Keane wiped his wet eyes and stood. He watched the ground for a long time. It had been a long time since he had seen them. Maura had died first and William a few years later.

Keane noticed how neat the grave site had been kept. He saw his uncle with the bluish-white cloud behind him standing at the gate. He took good care of his family, Keane thought. He felt a strong sense of relief as he stood at the grave of his parents.

How fortunate he felt to have found his family. He walked slowly to his uncle and met him at the gate.

"It's good to come home, isn't it, Paddy? Now you saw what you needed and 'tis time to move on now. I see you have a sense of wonder. That's a gift, son. It's a gift. Use it for yourself. Don't ever let the wonder cease, son." He put his hand on Keane's neck and gave it a shake.

"Now, let's go. You can visit here any time you wish."

They walked on.

"What are your plans for today, Patrick?"

"I've got to drive back to Ennistymon. I have my friend, Pauline, waiting to find out how my trip has gone."

"Haven't you called her?"

"No, no I haven't. So much has happened. I'm going to bring her back here to let everyone meet her."

"Grand. We'd all love to meet her now. Bring her Around and we'll chat some more. I'm going to visit

Kat'leén, your aunt, in the hospital now. Why don't you come along with me now, Patrick?"

The two men walked down the corridor toward Kathleen's room.

People passing by, personnel of the hospital, patients, and visitors, all knew Father Tommy Keane. Everyone said hello as they passed.

"Good morning, Kat'leen!"

"Good morning, Thomas. Patrick! Good of you to come." She sat up smiling.

"Come here, Patrick."

Keane bent toward Kathleen and kissed her.

"I went to the grave site this morning."

"The good Father watches over William and Maura."

She took Keane's hand.

"I'm glad you went. You needed to take care of that, right? Yes, you did."

"I'm going back to Ennistymon today. I am going to return with Pauline."

"Will you be gettin' married then, Patrick?" She smiled at her nephew.

"I've just met her this Summer. And..." He was cut off by the both of them.

"Why does that matter?" Kathleen said.

Father Keane pushed his hand through the air.

"Are ye a baby that you can't know what ye want?"

"Listen," Father Keane continued.

"If it is something you know for sure, then you get married. We can't wait to meet her, Patrick."

"Hopefully I'll be leaving here soon and I can meet her at home rather than as I am now."

"I love you." He told his aunt.

Words can be the softest touch. Kathleen's tears fell as those words brushed against her heart.

"I love ye, too, Patrick."

"I can't wait until we can all stop crying." Keane laughed.

"I've cried so much in these last days." He looked down, embarrassed.

"You've gone through much, Patrick. Tears cleanse the bad out." She said.

The three of them sat and spoke. Mostly it was Father Keane giving Kathleen the news of the Parish.

"You can get a position teaching in Ireland if you wanted." Father Keane said to Patrick as they went back to the small, white house.

"Live in Ireland?" Keane said.

"Of course! What about you and Pauline. S'pposin' it does work for the bot' of you. What then, Patrick? Back to Americay?"

He planted the seed just in case Keane thought nothing could grow.

"Well, yes, uhm, you are right. What if things are going to go well for Pauline and I?"

"Americay is a mighty big place, mighty big, indeed. But you've spent a lifetime lost. Will you now, after arriving at what you've wanted, go back taking Pauline from her home? Maybe, Patrick, maybe. If that's what ye want, go with God's blessing. But think about it clearly. Home is a wonderful place."

They pulled up in front of Maura's house.

"I'll be going back to the church now, son. Travel well. Please bring Pauline Around when you've come back."

He paused.

"We've missed you, son. I've missed you. We never knew what became of you. And all the time you've been trying to come back home. Go with God, Patrick. You look like your dad." He smiled.

Keane got out of the car and Father Keane pulled away. Maura was there at the door, smiling.

"Good morning to you again, Patrick."

"Hi. We've just seen Aunt Kathleen. She's feeling better."

"Grand. Are you hungry, Patrick? A cup of tea, maybe?"

"A cup of tea sounds fine, thanks. I'll be leaving after the tea. You have been so gracious to me coming unannounced as I have."

"Nonsense, Patrick. We've waited for you." She smiled at him again.

"Will you bring Pauline back with you now?"

She knew that was the reason for him leaving so soon. But she asked to remind him.

"I'd love to bring her here. I know she would love everyone as well." He took a sip of hot tea.

"Well then, go and get her and turn right around. We'll be waiting for ye." She said with a giggle.

"Thank you. That's what I'll do then." A big smile filled his face.

Keane saw the rise and fall of the familiar hills. The bright hues of green from the afternoon sun covered them. He felt all the wonder and excitement of what he found and of what he now had as his own.

Keane noticed the elation which he experienced at being back in the hills of Kilshanny. They enveloped him within their comforting slopes as he drove. He thought about the two places that became monumental for him at the close of all the stages of his journey. And his journey was closed now.

He thought about the words of Father Keane. Pauline was his beginning now. And he did come home.

He pulled the car quickly in front of Pauline's house, opened the door and hopped out. He went almost running to Pauline's door.

She opened it as he approached. Her arms went around him as to catch him as he came to her. They embraced and Pauline laughed loudly out of sheer happiness. The happiness that comes from so deep within about something so real and so filled with wonder.

"Oh Patrick!"

"I'm so happy you're here. I want to hear all about it. Come in and tell me, Pakie. I've missed you so."

They left each other's arms but still feeling the pull back to that embrace.

"I have found home. I found the house.

"And I have family, Pauline. And you're a part of it." He peered into her eyes.

Keane told Pauline of all the happenings in Kilashee. He told her about Maura and Michael Noonan. He told her about Kathleen. He described Father Keane to her and his pipe. He told her of his visit to the grave site.

"And we're going there tomorrow for an overnight visit. We must make the plans now. Everyone wants to meet you. Perhaps you can call John-Joe and Maeve and explain what has happened. What do you think? Will you go with me?"

"Yes, Patrick. Of course I will. I'll make the arrangements now."

She rose from her seat and went to the phone.

Pauline called Maeve first. She explained the situation at hand and Maeve was very understanding. Pauline needn't worry because Maeve could handle the breakfast.

John-Joe explained that it was very slow at the moment and he wouldn't need Pauline in the shop.

"When do we leave, Pakie?" She said as she put her arms around him. "Maeve sends her love, Pakie."

"We'll leave in the morning. It's a lovely drive. I'm so happy that you are with me." He kissed her.

The late afternoon settled into evening. A day relinquishes itself to night and dawn braves the surrender for day again. Each part abandoning its own strength for that of another's magnitude.

Keane surrendered to the journey as he surrendered to devotion in the small, white Kilshanny church. His life now moved in peaceful flows of life's waters.

Pauline had journeyed in her own way, as each life has its own identity. She surrendered letting the tight grip of her own strength slip free. She lived in peace, with herself, and with her surroundings. She knelt in church as her simplest form of humility displayed her contentment, peace, and well-being. There was no task involved. It was just Pauline's way of life. When she danced that day on Keane's long stone wall as he played his whistle she danced on the delicate ribbon that flows through her life. She had the sense of wonder which let her dance, which let her pray, which let her laugh her soft laugh. She was enraptured within the mystical stream of life. She knew that Keane had come to her on this very same mystical stream as it carried him on his journey. For the things which she did not have she never fretted. She knelt at church with peaceful resolve.

Keane had picked up Pauline's guitar and started to play quietly. Pauline was making them something to eat. Evening had settled outside with that glow of light.

Keane started to play New Horizons. Pauline joined in from the kitchen. Her voice mixing with Keane's as both sang in thankfulness and hope.

They ate their dinner in peace sealed off from the world. As the sky glowed from a light that should have dimmed. Pauline and Patrick were illuminated in a radiant union as they sat together. The union of two souls now entwined from their separate sojourns. The light of knowing glowed from their hearts as both sat across from each other. It was journey's end. It was meant to be.

"I don't have to return. I don't have to go back to America."

A great pause opened like sudden brightness.

"Patrick?" A light shone.

"I want to stay with you."

He was looking deeply into her eyes.

"I can see my life in front of me for the first time."

The gravity of the stare lightened as their eyes glistened with the deepest joy.

"Don't go, Patrick. Please don't go. I've never been happier and never more filled with joy."

She reached for his hand as she spoke the words.

Keane got up from the wooden chair and left the table. As he had done before on a different evening he put on a compact disc that Pauline enjoyed. It was Ritchie Havens' Follow.

He came back into the kitchen touched Pauline's hand as she rose from her chair.

Patrick slowly put his arms around Pauline's waist and they began to sway in gentle motion to the tune they both loved.

One song touched two hearts for so long and now they heard it together. And they held each other. The motion of their bodies moved in the summer glow of late evening light.

Patrick and Pauline held each other tightly while they danced. They moved, in a soft glow of light, silent, and their expressions were frozen with traces of joy. Her eyes, soft and beautiful, were staring into something they both knew and understood. His face held wonder. They were framed by the glow seeping in through the windows. No space lay between them. No time aged them. They did not belong anywhere but to this very moment. It was a soft burst of life's mercy.

Keane stopped the car at the top of the hill. He ran out and opened the door for Pauline.

"Have a look."

"It's right there. The small, white one."

Pauline might have guessed as there were not many homes in view.

"That's where I was born, Pauline. That's my house."

Keane stared at it himself as if for the first time.

Pauline was silent for a moment. She saw a part of Pakie's life appear and she took it in to herself.

"I can see you, Pakie." She laughed a light giggle.

"I mean, I can see you as a child, playing, riding your bicycle. I can see you, another part of you."

"Let's drive to the church to see Uncle Tommy." He suggested. "I want to see him first. With you I mean, Pauline. Maybe he's at the church."

The church was surrounded by meadows. The stone structure rose above the green. A black wrought-iron fence stood passively along the church ground. It neither kept people out or kept them in. It didn't guard or warn. The black wrought-iron fence just stood passively as a place within which was peace.

Keane pulled the car into the small lot adjacent to the church. He opened the door for Pauline.

Keane saw his Uncle's car. They walked over to the side door to where Father Thomas Keane had his office.

Keane knocked gently on the door.

"Hello, Patrick!

"And this must be Pauline!"

Father Keane smiled.

"She's lovelier than you told me about, Patrick.

"What a pleasure to meet you, Pauline."

He smiled and lifted his hand to place in hers.

But Pauline was overcome by meeting Keane's uncle. She reached for him with both arms and held him. She had tears forming in her eyes.

"Come, come, sit now." He led Pauline to a chair in his small office.

Pauline sat and Keane sat in the chair next to her.

Father Keane sat in his big leather chair. He reached for his well-used black pipe. He tapped it hard a few times on the palm of his hand.

"Pauline, I enjoy the puff of the pipe every now and again. Would that suit you now?"

He enjoyed the pipe more now than again.

"I don't mind at'tall, Father."

"Now."

Father Keane spoke clearly as he began to puff on his newly lit pipe.

"You're a Clare woman." He stated.

"Yes. I was born and raised in Kilshanny, Ennistymon."

"What a lovely part o' the country, Pauline."

He puffed on his pipe. The cloud of bluish-white smoke rose above his white hair.

"Are your parents in Kilshanny, Pauline?"

The questions were typical of his generation. The land and the family, a person's people, were important.

"No, Father. They're over in America. They've been there for just over fifteen years now. I was barely twenty when they'd gone. I couldn't leave Ennistymon. Dad's farm hadn't done well at the time. He had an offer from America. A relation of his had a growing business. I stayed on the farm in the house we own."

"I see, Pauline." Bluish-white smoke rose and gathered in a cloud.

"Have you seen them recently?" He said softly.

"No. Not recently. It's been nearly eight years now. They haven't much money to come home. They're well, though." She said in a low voice.

"Mmm. I understand, I do."

He peered into her eyes which momentarily met his before looking down. It was clear that she was upset.

"Now. Pauline. You're a lovely child. I can clearly see how Patrick has become enamored and enchanted with yourself. He couldn't help himself." He smiled and gave a small, short laugh.

"Now, Patrick. Will you be seeing your Aunt Kat'leen today?"

"Yes. I'll be going there after I walk to the grave."

"That's good. That's good. Send my regards. I'll be over today, too. Will I be seeing the bot' of you this evening at Maura and Michael's?"

"Yes. We'll be there." Keane answered.

"Ah good, good. It'll be a fine evening, sure. Good for the bot' of you."

Father Keane stood. His head veiled slightly in the cloud of blue smoke.

Pauline rose from the chair and Keane followed.

Thomas Keane came to Pauline. His arms went around the slender woman.

"Now, now, Pauline. Don't be worrying about anything. It's been our country's way for a long, sad time now."

"Stay strong now, Pauline. You're a fine woman."

"Thank you, Father." She said and then she smiled.

"That's it, now." He answered the smile.

Father Thomas Keane walked them both to the door and outside. He left them on the walk which led in one direction to the cemetery.

"Tonight, then."

He turned to go back into the church. Bluish-white smoke trailed behind him.

Pauline and Patrick turned and walked in the direction of the cemetery. Keane held Pauline's hand as they walked.

They stood silently over the grave of William and Maura Keane.

Keane knelt low and let his fingers trace their names in stone. William Patrick Keane. His Beloved Wife, Maura O'Boyle Keane. His hand dropped down to the ground resting on the dirt.

Pauline knelt next to Keane. She rested on the back of her legs as she put an arm across Keane's shoulders.

"They're back home, now." Keane almost whispered.

On the walk back to the car Keane asked about Pauline's parents.

"Maybe they can come out for the Christmas holidays." He said.

"We'll see, Pakie. We'll see." Her eyes looked down. She didn't speak any more about them.

They drove around the village of Kilashee having a look at the small community where Keane might have once lived.

They stopped at the hospital to visit Aunt Kathleen.

Patrick and Pauline walked into Aunt Kathleen's room. She was standing now near the side of the bed gathering things into a small bag.

She turned and saw the two of them.

"I'm going home, Patrick." Aunt Kathleen said with a big smile.

"And you must be Pauline. So very pretty. Patrick was in such a hurry to come and get you. I understand why." She said as she stepped toward Pauline.

"Hello, dear. I'm Patrick's Aunt Kat'leen. Long lost and found." She laughed as she hugged Pauline.

"We'll take you home, Aunt Kathleen." Keane offered.

"Oh that would be lovely. I can speak with Pauline then, as we go. But perhaps Maura is on her way."

"I'll give a call and check." Keane said.

Maura was at home. Keane explained that he and Pauline would be taking her mother home if that suited Maura.

"Grand, Patrick. We'll have some tea and lunch when you arrive." Maura said.

Patrick and Pauline attended to Aunt Kathleen as she gathered her things for going home. The nurses came with paperwork for the release of Aunt Kathleen and afterward the three of them went on their way.

"You're a Clare woman, Pauline?" Aunt Kathleen asked as the three of them drove back to the small, white house.

Pauline covered a giggle so as not to be rude. She didn't mind the questions. She knew that these were the questions of that generation for whom it meant so much. Family is the most important possession that is both possessed and possesses at the same time. Land and family, belonging both to love and to be loved.

"Yes, I'm from County Clare. I was born and reared in Kilshanny of Ennistymon. It's in west Clare."

"Very good. It's good to come from somewhere and to know from where it is you do come." Aunt Kathleen spoke from what she knew.

"I'm so happy, dear, that you've joined us. Everyone is so excited about Patrick being back with us. Have you met Maura and Michael?"

"I haven't, no." Pauline said in a quiet voice.

"I've met Father Keane, though." She added.

"Ah sure, 'tis a good man, there, Pauline. That's Patrick's uncle, on his dear father's side.""

"Pakie, you've got to let Father Keane know that you're taking Aunt Kat'leen home."

"Oh yea, thanks, Pauline. We'll stop now to see if he's in."

Keane drove to the church to see if his uncle's car was still parked outside. It was and he saw Uncle Tommy out for his walk. The cloud of bluish-white smoke following behind as he stepped.

Keane pulled up next to his uncle and greeted him.

"Uncle Tommy, good afternoon."

"Hello Patrick! How are ye?" He stopped walking.

"I've got Aunt Kathleen with us. She's going home now."

"Ah, good, good." He stepped around to Aunt Kathleen.

"Hello Kat'leen. 'Tis good to have you out of the sick room. Welcome home." He smiled and touched her arm through the open window.

"Hello Thomas. How are you keepin'?

"And will you be over for dinner and conversation tonight? It's a big night what with Pauline from Clare with us and Patrick, too."

"I'll be there, Kat'leen, please God."

"Ah sure, I'll be there. We'll sing some songs then. I'll have to dig out some Clare songs for the lovely Pauline." He laughed.

Pauline smiled at him.

"What you don't remember, Father, I'll be singing for you, sure." Pauline said.

"God bless to you all. I'll see you tonight. Glad to have you out, Kat'leen." He gently patted her arm.

They drove away from the church to the small, white house in which Keane was born.

"Hello mum!" Maura said from the door of the house as Keane opened the car door for Aunt Kathleen.

Maura walked down to greet her mother giving her a hug as she came close. She had noticed Pauline, of course, and when she gave her mother a hug she walked over to Pauline, too.

"Hi Pauline. So glad you've come." She hugged Pauline tightly.

"Do you need to rest, mum?" Maura asked as she grabbed a bag and let her mother hold her arm as they walked to the house.

"I'll have a cup o' tea, dear, please." Kathleen said.

Maura sat her mother down on the couch in the living room. Patrick sat next to her as Pauline walked into the kitchen to help Maura with the tea.

Maura smiled at Pauline.

"Pauline everyone will be so glad to meet you."

She held Pauline's arm momentarily.

"Thank you. Can I give a hand with the tea?" Pauline asked. Her smile was framed by her long dark hair hanging down below her shoulders.

"Now."

She handed Pauline some cups and saucers.

They drank their tea in the living room. Patrick Keane sat next to Kathleen O'Boyle Lynch, his mother's sister. On his other side Maura sat with Pauline in the middle. All the connections to life were present. Family to family, heart to heart, under one close roof.

Next to Keane now were Father Thomas Keane on his father's side and then Kathleen O'Boyle Lynch with Maura on her side. Michael Noonan sat next to his wife, Pauline next to Patrick next to Uncle Tommy. Maura's boys sat in the chairs in a branch of the circle. It was later in the evening and tea was still being served after dinner.

We need a tune." Uncle Tommy said.

"Let's see." Keane said.

Pakie took out his whistle and played the air that he played so many times at his place on the long, stone wall in Kilshanny.

Everyone listened to the music. Even the younger boys had an appreciation of the music that covered a land as certain as the hills.

"Grand!" Uncle Tommy said at the end of the tune.

Keane didn't miss a beat and kept it going with a reel. He was tapping his foot quickly as he spun the notes out of the metal tube of the whistle.

Hand clapping came at the end of the reel. Michael had gotten up to get his concertina. He began some Longford reels and some Kilashee jigs.

The music rolled on. Scones and tea were put out on a tray.

Pauline sang some Clare songs. Her voice soft and gentle reaching out to the yearning soul. She sang without musical accompaniment.

As the music and the generations met more relations gathered into the small, white house. Kathleen O'Boyle Lynch let everyone know of the celebration as she assembled the clan to welcome back Patrick Keane, of William and Maura Keane, of Kilashee. The living room was full of people, Keane's people. And the woman from Clare smiled at her man. And the man from Kilshanny smiled back through the generations that gathered to welcome him home.

The music filled the room and the house as the people played their Longford and Kilashee tunes.

Bodhrans, whistles, flutes, concertinas, and accordions all gathered as the music of the people played to celebrate a life. The music was played to celebrate all of life. This was the heart of music. Music seeks out in wondrous manifestations of sadness, happiness, and joy as a river reaches out in streams and brings life. The soul is lifted by the sound of music.

Keane was in the middle of all the people that have been here waiting for him to come home. He stood in the middle of the stream wading while taking in all that life had for him. The music went on. The stream flowed. Pauline glanced at Patrick and he back at her and they became one through a smile stretched across the face of the room.

Life is the length of the river run.

The morning did come eventually and Keane found Father Thomas Keane walking the same steps in his meditation around the church yard. A trail of bluish- white smoke formed as Father Keane puffed on his pipe.

When all was said and done and the tune was over this is where Father Thomas Keane was at home.

"Good morning, Uncle Tommy."

"Ah, good morning, son. Lovely day, ^{A}tisn't it?" He said as Keane began to match his steps.

"You really played a great whistle last night, Uncle Tommy."

"'Twas a grand night. These are your people, Patrick. They all came out for you. They were caught up in the stream, Patrick."

They walked along the yard of the church which bordered the cemetery. Father Thomas Keane looked over toward it.

"I see you've got an Irish name given to you by Miss Pauline." Uncle Tommy laughed.

"Pakie." Father Keane added.

"Well, really it was given to me by Maeve O'Connor the proprietor of Tullamore Farmhouse where I'm staying."

"I've known a few Pakie's. All good men.

"Are you stayin' Pakie? I mean to say, now, are ye staying in Ireland. I'm sure you can see it's home for you. But you must make up your own mind. All your people are here, son. Settle down now." Father Keane told him.

The two men walked the length of the church yard in the morning sun. Behind the priest and the man a trail of bluish-white smoke created small clouds before disappearing. But ahead of the priest and the man, all was clear.

14

Home

The hills of Kilshanny extended out around Keane. Once again. Their rise and fall filled his vision and stretched his steps as he walked. There was never a place like this that he could remember. Like the hills around him his thoughts had a rise and fall to them as he went over the events of the last few days. Keane was glad to be in the hills again walking the narrow, bony road. He shared his thoughts in silence with the hills.

He needed the quiet rejoinder from the soft green hues of the rise and fall of the quilted, ancient earth. His slow, stretched- out stride went passed the bones of stone walls which carved the green pastures in his path. He heard his answer whispered then.

He walked passed Pauline's house until he stopped a distance away.

"Good morning, Patrick." John-Joe said in his cheery voice.

"How are you keepin'?" He asked Keane.

"I'm well, thanks, John-Joe." Keane said standing on the porch of his home.

John-Joe pushed the door open wider and invited Keane into his home.

"I'm glad you could make it, Patrick. You're right on time."

Keane went into John-Joe's house. His wife was out at the market working. The day starts early at the fruit and vegetable market in Ennistymon.

Both men sat at the long, wooden kitchen table. John-Joe put on tea and when it was ready he placed the hot cups down in front of them. He pushed a plate of brown bread toward Keane.

"Thanks." Keane reached for the bread and took a big bite and then a sip of tea.

"Everything's in order, Patrick. We can finish it up now and have the papers go through town and in a short time we'll have it official, like."

"Oh, that's wonderful. I'm so pleased about it all. I feel it's the best and I certainly appreciate all of your help and willingness in the matter."

He took a sip of tea and another hungry bite of the thick brown bread.

"Ah, sure, you're certainly welcome, Patrick. It's been a pleasure. I know it will serve you well in the near future. And it's nothing I'll be needing."

Keane handed some of his own paperwork to John-Joe and John-Joe took it and left the table. He came back a few minutes later.

"We're set, then, Patrick." He stood and reached for Keane's hand and shook it with a firm hand.

Keane stayed and chatted with John-Joe a few minutes. He finished his tea and then said goodbye.

Keane walked down the narrow, bony road passed Pauline's home. She wasn't at home, of course, she was at Tullamore. It was done now. Like Abraham and the Hittites Keane buried his past and was an alien no longer.
The strength of knowing when something was right lay deep within him. And he walked on in his final stage of journey.

"I've made some phone calls about it, Kay." Paul said loudly to his wife who was standing at the top of the staircase.

"And it seems quite possible to do it, dear. It just may happen for us as we are wanting."

Paul sat at his desk balancing out finances for examination. Their retirement would come soon.

"I think something will turn up for us unexpectedly and we'll manage." Kay spoke ever hopeful as was her way.

Paul and Kay spoke with Keane earlier in the morning. Keane had phoned from Pauline's to tell them all about the events in Kilashee.

This conversation spurred Paul on to check on things in Ennistymon. He called the contacts he had made there. He started their search. Paul and Kay wanted deeply to settle in Kilshanny at retirement. They loved Ennistymon and felt it was home for them.

Keane walked through the black wrought iron gate. It felt as if much time had passed since he last stepped into the Kilshanny church. But it hadn't been that much time except for that which a lifetime could hold. That is what just passed before Keane these last few days. It was a lifetime. Now things slowed and stopped as he went into the sanctuary.

After some time Father Kelly came out. He walked quickly toward Keane with his arm out slightly pointing as if reaching for something.

"Patrick. Patrick Keane!" Father Kelly was almost yelling.

Keane came out of the pew and walked toward Father Kelly meeting him by the alter.

"If you have a moment I'd like to speak with you." He had his hand resting on Keane's arm.

"Good morning, Father. Yes, I have the time now."

Father Kelly led Keane toward a side door of the sanctuary leading into his office.

He showed Keane a chair and then sat behind his desk.

"First, Patrick, let me tell you that I am very happy for you in finding your family in Kilashee."

He looked at Keane waiting for his expression of surprise. He didn't wait long.

"I had a conversation with Father Thomas Keane of Kilashee." He smiled.

"He informed me of your trip back to County Longford. We spoke, Patrick, about your staying. Neither he nor I want to pry into your life. But, if you do want to stay, and I should tell you, you would be greatly missed by many and one in particular if you do not stay, I am in need of a teacher. Now, it's not a seminary, but the school is a good one and I think you would rather enjoy it. Father Thomas Keane also thinks it would benefit you. It's one of our schools up in Lisdoonvarna. It would be grand if you accepted. We are ready for just before September to get you acquainted and then start in earnest in September." Father Kelly looked hopefully at Keane.

Pauline hung up the phone with Maeve. She had been asking for Patrick. Maeve hadn't seen him all day. Pauline hadn't seen him all day, either. She hadn't seen him since breakfast at Tullamore. She walked over to the window not expecting to see him come up the walk but went to the window to look out knowing he was well.

She stepped to the cabinet nearby and pressed a button. The song they both loved, the song by which they held each other close and danced, came on. And she waited.

Standing by the window singing with the song she heard a car rushing nearer to her home. It was Keane's car. He pulled up quickly. She smiled and went to the door. He jumped out of the car and with a slight run came to the door where Pauline stood waiting.

"Hello Pakie. I didn't want to worry." She smiled at him.

"But I did." She laughed a small, gentle laugh.

"Hello Pauline. I've missed you this long day."

He came to her with his arms out and hugged her tightly. He didn't let go and like the sun in the evening sky his hold lingered with a glow.

Keane heard the song playing. He hummed it. He pulled slightly away from Pauline. It was just enough of a distance to look at her face and to kiss her.

They walked into the house. Pauline led him into the kitchen for something to eat. She knew he'd be hungry. She placed plates on the table and got things ready.

"Well, young man. Where have you gone to all day?"

"You're going to find out right now. Or perhaps after dinner. Which?" He asked her with a laugh.

Pauline stopped what she was doing.

"It'll be this very moment that you'll tell me."

"Now."

"Then come here."

He stood and brought her into the living room. He started the song again. The song they both loved.

"Pauline."

He peered into her eyes. He paused to calm himself.

"I've got a position with the church. Father Kelly spoke with me this morning. My uncle had called him and spoke to him about my staying. I've agreed to take the position. It's as a teacher in the school up in Lisdoonvarna. I'll be starting soon. Officially in September."

"' Let the river rock you like a cradle.'" The song sang out it's lines.

"Oh Patrick. That's grand. It's wonderful. I'm so happy."

Her arms went around him as he sat. She wiped the beginning of a tear away. She knew this meant so much to him.

Patrick Thomas Keane looked at Pauline O'Sullivan.

"What Patrick? What is it?"

"Pauline. I have one more thing to say. And I want to say it now."

He looked at her. Then he stood and went to his jacket pocket. He came back to her.

"Pauline. All the words I could ever say at this moment will never meet what you've brought to my life. I knew it was you from the first time you tapped so gently on my door. And now I've come to this point at the end of my long journey."

He looked at her as if looking beyond her to a future where this question would come to rest.

Pauline sat with her hands folded on her lap afraid to move. Afraid that any sudden movement might jolt her back to when she was without him. She sat as if the steadiness of this moment was dependent on her sitting as still as possible to keep everything in its place.

He reached for her hands resting them on her lap nestling her small, gentle hands protectively within his own.

"Pauline will you marry me?"

And he stopped speaking. He stopped moving. He sat as still as she as if now the moment was resting on him to keep all the future aligned.

He placed a small, delicate box in her hands resting in her lap.

"Pakie! Patrick!"

She lurched forward throwing the dependency of the moment that was upon her moments before, throwing it away to care for itself. This was a new moment. A moment that only needed to rest on her words.

"Yes, Patrick Keane. I will marry you."

"Of course I will. How could I never do it?"

She burst out with the tears that had been swelling behind her eyes.

She touched the box with care and opened it slowly.

She looked in it and cried more tears. Keane took the ring out and placed it on her finger.

Some words have an echo. Some words have gravity and the sheer weight of them beckons their repetition. Her words kept circling in his mind.

"Yes."

"Of course."

"How could I never do it?"

Pauline was holding him with her arms clasped about his neck with the intention of never letting go. For the both of them this moment was bigger than any moment. They had both endured so many years of loneliness. It was the loneliness of waiting. Now the waiting was over. The two rivers of life met and became one flowing river of peace.

Keane stood bringing Pauline to her feet with his movement. He pressed the button. The song played. He followed. She followed. They were in the same step.

They danced so slowly to the tune they both loved. No other thing in all the world existed at this moment but the two of them. And the song carried them gently as they kissed.

"Let the river rock you like a cradle."

Life is the length of the river run.

Keane arrived back at Tullamore very late after midnight. It seemed for hours they danced and held each other. He wanted to close his eyes and sleep but the moments that had transpired did not allow sleep. They allowed only thoughts. All the years of loneliness and now in a moment what was once alone has been swept away replaced by his family, his friends, and now, by Pauline, who will be his wife. He thought of life with her and it was a peaceful, gentle feeling. He slept then, thinking of Pauline.

He awoke after awhile and got out of the warm bed. After getting ready he left the house and walked his most familiar steps. Down the long farmhouse road and over the white wood and stone bridge. The sheep were out in the pasture. The narrow, bony road lifted high over the rise and fall of the hills with a quilt of soft green upon the ancient backs. He saw the spire of the church reaching out of the hues of green. The narrow, bony road turned and turned yet again always with the hills at its sides and even under its narrow, bony surface.

Keane arrived at the church stopping at the wrought iron gate. He went in.

"I won't come alone any more." He thought to himself.

"But I had to come this last time like this. Like the first time. Now it's complete. Now its complete." He thought.

He walked then to Pauline's home. The dogs were out by the large barn. The men were inside working. He went deep into the valley down the dirt road. He walked above the pastures which lifted him. He stopped at where the road turned toward Pauline's home. He stared out to the land that invited him. He felt the Akubra on his head. But that was gone. Things have changed. He smiled and walked on. He passed his place, the long stone wall where Pauline danced and he played. So many days and hours had been spent at this gate. He walked on.

Pauline opened the door and let Keane in.

"This is where I belong."

That's what Keane said when he stepped into Pauline's home. He held her and said those words. His face had the look of all the years without Pauline. And at that moment he felt the tiredness of being without her. But deep within himself the well of comfort was rising to the surface. The landscape within had changed to that of belonging.

Keane sat in the private kitchen of Maeve eating his breakfast. Pauline poured him more coffee and then went out to the dining room to see what was needed by the other guests.

Maeve was cooking the breakfast and getting everything ready for Pauline to take out to the dining room. John was sitting in his chair on the other side near the television and the wood burning stove.

"How are you keepin', Pakie?" Maeve turned and smiled at her guest.

"I'm well, thanks. I'm getting married." He said it out loud.

"I thought I saw a ring on Pauline's finger!" Maeve exclaimed with a broad smile.

"And one that I had never seen her wear before!"

Maeve noticed the ring right away this morning. She didn't say anything to Pauline or Patrick.

"I wasn't sure, now, if it was the ring that gave it away to me or was it her smile this morning. She had the most glorious glow as she came through the door. She was telling all the world without saying a word." Maeve laughed aloud.

She came and sat next to Keane.

Maeve watched the whole romance nurture and grow. She watched the both of them from the very first day. The way they looked at each other. The secret smiles. Then the touching, her hand to his shoulder, or her hand to his hand, first so innocent while trying to hide it. And then they were just always together.

Maeve put her hand on his. She looked at him as a mother would a son.

"I think it's wonderful, Pakie. I think it's so wonderful. What a time! What a time you've had coming to Ireland."

Keane laughed. It was quite a time. He had already explained all the events of Kilashee to Maeve and John.

"Father Kelly has offered me a position teaching."

"In Lisdoonvama?" She asked.

"Yes. At their school."

John O'Connor got up out of his chair and came to Keane.

"Congratulations, son. Pauline is a fine woman. A fine Clare woman."

He put his hand on Keane's shoulder. Then he reached to shake his hand.

"She's a fine woman, indeed. And you're alright yourself, sure." John said as he let out a laugh.

"Pakie, things are really working out for you now. It's so exciting to have watched it all unfold before me very eyes. And to think it happened right here. Right here at Tullamore." She got up shaking her head. She had to get back to cooking breakfast.

"We'll all have to sit and talk about it, Pakie. If you don't mind. I do want to hear all about it. We'll celebrate." She said. She was smiling happily.

Pauline walked through the private kitchen entrance carrying empty plates and tea cups. She stepped passed Keane, turned toward him in a quick spin, and smiled. Keane's eyes lit up reflecting Pauline's happiness. He smiled back at her.

"That's a lovely ring you've got on, Pauline. Is it new? I've never seen it." Maeve said and then turned to Keane with a wink.

Pauline looked quickly at Keane not knowing what to say.

"Oh you have a new ring? When did you get it?" Keane quipped.

"Pakie!"

"I've just told Maeve we're getting married. But she knew already."

"Pauline!" Maeve exclaimed.

"I'm so happy for ye. You know that I am."

In a quieter, gentler voice Maeve continued.

"I love you, Pauline. God bless you." She cried.

She took a step to Pauline and put her arms around her.

"This is some occasion, young lady." Maeve said sniffling.

Later in the afternoon Pauline and Patrick telephoned Paul and Kay in England to tell them the news of their engagement.

"Hello Paul. It's Patrick."

"Patrick. Brilliant that you've called. It seems as if you'll never leave Ireland, Patrick. You've been there for so long now." Paul laughed.

"Paul. I've got some news."

Paul turned serious and listened.

"Yes, Patrick. Are you alright?"

"I'm wonderful. Can Kay listen in now?"

"Of course." He called for Kay to pick up another phone.

"Hello, Patrick." Kay said.

"Hi Kay. I've got some news."

"Pauline and I are going to be married."

"Patrick!" Paul and Kay said it together.

"Patrick! That is grand. I'm so excited I almost don't know what to say." Paul said.

"Patrick, I wish you and Pauline all the best of everything. God bless the both of you." Kay said.

"Patrick, of course. Congratulations! God bless, of course. This is such a happy moment for all of us. Thank you for letting us know." Paul said.

"Father Kelly at the Kilshanny church has offered me a teaching position in Lisdoonvarna. I'll be staying in Ireland."

"Oh my, Patrick. You are the news today, aren't you?" Paul said.

"Patrick, let me speak with Pauline." Kay said.

"Pauline, how happy you must be right now. You two are so wonderful together."

Kay went on and spoke with Pauline.

Pauline went on about the ring and how it happened. She spoke in excited tones.

When they hung up with Paul and Kay the two of them sat in the silence of the day looking out on the hues of green surrounding the home. The late afternoon drifted into the evening with its glow lightly streaming through the windows. The sun was setting earlier now. It didn't stretch its light so far any longer. The summer was setting, too. Tullamore sat on the hill that was home. The last flush of evening light rested atop the long farmhouse road. The Terebinth tree could be seen extending its protective branches over the high pasture near the door of Tullamore.

They sat in his office watching the cloud of bluish-white smoke rise above his white hair.

"Your church means much to you, I understand, Pauline. And Father Kelly is your pastor. A kind and gentle man is he, too."

Father Thomas Keane paused for a moment. Then he answered their question which was the reason they came to him.

"I'm honored to marry the bot' of you. It will be arranged." He puffed on his pipe as Pauline smiled.

"I'll wait a day or so before calling Father Kelly and making the arrangements. This will give you time to go and speak with him yourselves about your plans. I see no problem with it. I know he'll understand. Now. It's settled. Let's have a walk then." He stood and his head rose above the cloud of bluish-white smoke.

Father Thomas Keane would marry them. Pauline had suggested it to Keane. She thought it would be good for Keane to have his father's brother marry them. Keane suggested the Kilshanny church since it, too, would mean that Pauline would be at home. It was agreed and they had driven to Kilashee to speak with Father Keane.

Father Kelly held Pauline's hand as he smiled warmly congratulating the both of them.

"The Kilshanny church is your home, Pauline. It's your church. Of course we will use it for your wedding day. And Patrick, how wonderful to have your uncle come down and perform the ceremony. It will be a wonderful day."

15

You Are Not Alone

The next day Keane awoke early as he always had done. He hurried more than usual this morning, though. He left the house and walked carrying a small canvas bag. When he arrived at where the dirt road turned toward Pauline's home Keane scrambled through the high hedges lining the land.

He walked far out into the pasture and stopped. It was almost center.

He dropped the canvas bag down on the land and knelt to open it. He took out the wooden stakes and cord that he needed.

He hammered in one stake and tied the cord tightly to it. He stood and let out some cord and walked to where he needed to walk and stopped. He drove another stake into the ground and tied the cord to this one. He paced out more steps until he marked a huge square of land. He looked at it all and smiled.
The wind off of the ocean blew through his hair as he stood guard over his land.

"Pauline! Pauline!" He yelled at the door. He hadn't yet knocked. He just yelled excitedly for Pauline.

She opened the door in a flash of movement.

"Patrick! Are you alright? What's the matter?"

"Let's go. Come with me. Hurry, I need to show you something. Come on!"

Keane didn't give her any time to think. But she did turn quickly and grab her jacket that was hanging near the door.

"Patrick, what is it? What is it?"

"Come on, Pauline. What a fine morning it tis!" He laughed as he grabbed her hand and he took off running.

Pauline and Patrick ran down the empty, narrow, bony road to the end. He took her where no hedges stood in the way and ran them both onto the great pasture. He stopped.

"What, Patrick? What's going on?" Pauline felt the excitement of the moment but still did not know what it was all about.

Keane walked her to where the stakes were marking the land. He stepped over the cord and she followed him.

They stood in the center facing the ocean which was beyond the next low-lying hill. The wind captured them and blew through their hair.

"This is beautiful here, Pauline. I love it so very much."

"You have to let me know if you feel the same way. Is it beautiful, Pauline? Is it beautiful to you, too?"

"Patrick. I love it. You know I love Kilshanny. We took Paul and Kay back here. I told you then I loved this piece of land. It's a most wonderful place to have a home."

She looked around her and took in all the beauty that the land offered.

"Pauline. This is my gift to you. I've purchased this land from John-Joe. He hadn't any use of it any longer and I asked about it. It's our land, Pauline. It's our land."

Pauline looked at him with wide eyes. She glanced around her at all the stakes marking the land.

"Oh my, Pakie. I can't believe it. I can't believe all the things that have happened." She stepped closer to him.

"Believe, Pauline. As I have believed. As you have taught me to believe."

"Oh Pakie! Is this where our home will be? Will we build on it, Pakie?" She said excitedly. The reality was hitting her now.

"This morning I came early and marked off a section to show you. The builder must come and do a proper marking. But this is the general idea of where our home will be. We'll build a home here and live."

Pauline stepped in closer to him and held his hand. They both faced the ocean as the wind went through them. The two figures stood in the midst of hues of green with all of their dreams staked out. The wind blew but they did not move. They just stood closer with only warmth between them. They stared at the ground, at the stakes, at the sky reaching for the ocean and the land.

Pauline led Patrick around the borders of their land slowly. She went from corner to corner until completing the marked off area.

Pauline leaped toward Keane and hugged him with all of her strength. She started to jump up and down with happiness.

"Catch me, Pakie. Catch me!"

And she ran through her new home yelling out the names of the different rooms as she ran.

"I'm in the kitchen, Pakie. Catch me. I'm in the living room, you can't find me!" She screamed, laughed and ran through the house.

"Guess where I am now, Pakie?" She laughed and stopped still.

Keane caught her there. And he kissed her there.

September came and Patrick Keane started his teaching position. He taught religion at the Catholic secondary school in Lisdoonvarna. He lived at Tullamore which would close at the end of September. Maeve would not let Patrick

Keane move elsewhere. They made the arrangements for him to live there until the new house would stand.

There would be a December wedding. Pauline wanted a Christmas wedding and Keane loved the idea. Pauline stayed busy making arrangements, simple as she wanted them. Keane went to work each day and then back to Tullamore and then to Pauline's home. Life found a rhythm for them both as each day was built onto the next.

The river flowed peacefully in their lives nourishing their needs. Peace was the river and it did stream through Pauline and Patrick.

The summer would always be with them but a newer time began now. The holiday that was journey was over and life began for Pauline and Patrick. Tullamore was still high on the hill but it looked and felt different for Keane. He couldn't have been a more fortunate man. He said so in his prayers. He and Pauline would kneel in the pew come Sunday mornings. The pew in the front not hiding from anything.

Time went on as a river always does with its constant flow. September turned to October turning again to November and pausing there just before December. But December came nonetheless. December came nonetheless.

"Pauline! Pauline!" Keane yelled as he had that one day to show Pauline the land.

"Pauline! Pauline!"

It was a Wednesday afternoon.

"Patrick! What is it? What have you done now?" She laughed. She leaned at the door and kissed him hello.

"Come with me. We're going for a ride. There's something I have to do. I want you to come along with me."

Pauline grabbed her coat and they went to Keane's car. He had to purchase one as he returned the rental car back in the summer.

He opened the door for Pauline and then got in himself. He drove away and out to the national road. After some time they were in Shannon.

"What are we doing in Shannon, Pakie?"

"We have to go to the airport."

She tried to get the information but Keane was silent. He parked the car at Shannon airport and they got out and walked to the doors.

They walked up the long corridors to where the passengers would be getting off of the plane.

"Patrick! What's going on? Please tell me." She begged him.

"We'll wait here. You'll know soon, Pauline. I promise. I'm sorry to do it like this but it's a surprise." He kissed her and held her hand.

The people started to stream from the plane and flow into the passenger waiting area. The stream of people rushed passed the two of them until Pauline saw what Keane wanted her to see.

"Mum! Mum!" Pauline screamed with tears.

"Dad! Dad!" She cried hard now.

"Oh Patrick! Oh Patrick! Thank you!" And she ran to her parents. They embraced her and they all cried.

Keane watched the family reunite after so many years. They needed to be with one another. They were her parents. The three of them hugged for a long time and everyone cried.

Pauline turned to Patrick and saw him standing alone in the distance. He saw her face framed by her beautiful hair. Tears were streaming down her face as she looked at him.

"Patrick! Come here with us!" She called out to him.

Keane walked over to the three of them. Pauline hugged him bringing him into the fold of family.

Keane only spoke to them on the phone. He had arranged it with the help of Father Kelly.

Pauline 'turned to Patrick and hugged him separately.

"Thank you, Pakie." She whispered.

They returned to Pauline's home. Everyone got out

of the car and her parents stopped to look once again at their home. It was dark now. The summer sun was gone. But still her parents stood in the cold of evening looking at where they once belonged.

It snowed that day. Christmas Day brought snow which covered the ground in its pure white blanket. It doesn't snow that much in Ireland. But it did on Christmas Day. It was Pauline's Wedding day, too. She looked out of her window and saw the white covering. She smiled upon seeing all the freshness of the day.

Keane readied himself that morning. Father Thomas Keane was at Tullamore. As well as Michael and Maura Noonan with their two boys. Aunt Kathleen was there, too. There were other relations there as well. Maeve's house was full. Tullamore was active once again.

Tullamore was bustling with people getting ready. Maura sat at the piano in the front sitting room. She played the brightest hymns with the loveliest voice. No one minded that this day was Christmas. It's different in Ireland. It's not so much about gifts as it is about people, as it is about family. Every one was happy to be present for this happiest of occasions.

Patrick Keane rode to Kilshanny Church with Father Thomas Keane. They parked at the wrought iron fence.

"I know your parents are watching and with us, Patrick." He grabbed Keane's hand and shook it.

They got out of the car and went through the gate and into the door and entered the sanctuary.

Father Kelly having given Mass this Christmas morning now sat at the piano and sang a hymn.

Everyone was gathered. Everyone was in the sanctuary. Maeve and John sat up close with Paul and Kay and Pauline's parents.

Father Thomas Keane celebrated the wedding Mass. When it was time Pauline came down the aisle. Music played from the piano as Father Kelly played and watched Pauline at the same time.

Keane looked at her. He breathed in deeply. Of course she was more beautiful than ever before. This moment would stay with Keane always.

Father Thomas Keane stood with Pauline and Patrick at the alter and the ceremony began. It was a simple and meaningful gathering. The words filled the air and hung protectively over them. The hues of green were covered with white. The hills rose and fell around Kilshanny with a new covering of white snow.

And Pauline and Patrick were married.

Father Kelly played the piano now and sang Peace is Flowing like a River. It was Keane's favorite hymn. Father Kelly had remembered.

Patrick leaned into Pauline. He kissed her as his wife. Pauline Keane stood before her husband and cried with such happiness that it could not be compared. The new snow covered everything outside of the sanctuary. Father Kelly played the hymn. Everyone joined in the hymn now. The sanctuary filled with the gentle sound of this most beautiful tune. The voices filled everyone's heart and for no reason everyone stood while they sang.

Pauline and Patrick walked down the aisle and stood at the door of the Kilshanny church. They looked at the snow that covered everything. The hymn was still heard. The hills were so quiet now. They were so peaceful and still in the snow.

Paul and Kay came first and congratulated them both. They lived in Kilshanny now. They found a lovely home near Pauline's house. Everyone was in their place now. Peace was flowing like a river.

Father Thomas Keane drove Pauline and Patrick Keane to the end of the snow covered dirt road which didn't just turn toward Pauline's house any longer. There was a small extension built onto the end now. Father Thomas Keane drove onto this small drive. He stopped in front of their new home. It was placed near where Keane had driven the stakes into the ground.

Father Keane opened the door for Pauline and kissed her. He shook Keane's hand.

"God bless you both. We'll see you soon."

He got into the car and drove away.

Pauline and Patrick walked to the door of their new home and entered. They stood at the door and looked out on all the new snow.

"I love you, Patrick."

Slowly Pauline closed the door.

It was a few days later that Father Thomas Keane walked passed the grave site of William and Maura Keane. He swept the snow away.

As Father Thomas Keane walked a cloud of bluish-white smoke rose behind him. He thought about Abraham. He thought about Pauline and Patrick. He thought about all that had occurred. He turned and walked into the church.

"Life is the length of the river run."

www.ingramcontent.com/pod-product-compliance
Lightning Source LLC
Chambersburg PA
CBHW071649090426
42738CB00009B/1469